The Salvation Controversy

G. Michael Cocoris

The Salvation Controversy

G. Michael Cocoris

INSIGHTS FROM THE WORD
2016 Euclid St. #20
Santa Monica, CA 90405
310-396-3132
www.insightsfromtheword.com

In memory of Jack Moulton,
a dear friend,
who was committed to grace,
especially the preaching of the cross

© 2008 by
G. Michael Cocoris

ISBN: 978-0-615-24245-3

Cocoris, G. Michael
    The Salvation Controversy

Printed in the United States by Morris Publishing
3212 East Highway 30
Kearney, NE 68847
1-800-650-7888

TABLE OF CONTENTS

FOREWORD

As a young pastor, 52 years ago, I invited Haddon Robinson, a friend from college days, to come to our church for one of his early evangelistic meetings. Our little church was packed as he served spiritual food for both the regenerate and the unregenerate. For me, it was a life-changing experience from zeal without knowledge to a balance of enthusiastic knowledge as I listened to his careful exposition of the free grace of God (Rom. 3:24) to which our people gave rapt attention.

As we spent hours together, I asked him how he learned such exposition of Scripture and he offered to show me by turning me to James 1:19-25 to develop my first expository message "How to Listen to a Sermon": The preparation before the message, the participation during the message, and the practice after the message. (Later in seminary I learned that it was an outline from Howard Hendricks). But my appetite had been whetted and he strongly encouraged me to attend seminary again: this time at a seminary founded by Lewis Sperry Chafer where they specialized in the teachings of the grace of God.

Two faculty members in particular, Dr. Charles Ryrie and Professor Zane Hodges, were used by God to clarify what I would call justification salvation and sanctification salvation. Faith alone in Christ alone by grace alone plus nothing brings the free gift of everlasting life, the declaration of the believer's righteousness, and the regeneration by the Holy Spirit. But the stewardship of that life requires our best efforts and commitment if we are to earn the rewards that Jesus Christ desires to give to all believers at the time of the Bema which will determine our capacity to magnify Christ in our reign with Him in glorification salvation. Dr. Jody Dillow has written powerfully about this in his book *The Reign of the Servant Kings* (Dan. 7:18, 26-27). The spread of this message was heralded worldwide through the pulpit and radio ministry of Dr. J. Vernon

McGee of the famous Church of the Open Door and he was succeeded at that church by the author of this book, *The Salvation Controversy*, by Dr. Mike Cocoris. It was in his ministry at C.O.D. that Mike and I became close friends and I witnessed the clarity of both his pulpit ministry and writing skills. In 1987, when I was given the task of developing the Nelson Study Bible (now called *The NKJV Study Bible*), I selected 40 authors. Dr. Cocoris was one of them and all of them had only one book for which to develop study notes except for Dr. Cocoris. Over the ten year period (1987 to 1997) I found myself calling on Dr. Cocoris to rewrite and clarify the notes of several books of the Bible because of his clarity and precision as well as his practical application.

When I read the manuscript of *The Salvation Controversy* I encountered the same skills that I have found in his other books as well as *The Nelson Study Bible* (now called *The NKJV Study Bible*). One very helpful clarification that brought joy to my heart related to the ongoing discussion that we are experiencing among free grace students and writers. We who are united in our belief about faith alone in Christ alone plus nothing have not yet been able to come to agreement about the minimum that must be believed in order to receive everlasting life. Some believe that John 20:31 is sufficient and others believe that the hermeneutic of progress of revelation would require more such as the death and resurrection of Christ. But whatever side we may take in that issue, we all agree that we are commanded to preach the death and resurrection of Christ along with the Apostle Paul who said "we preach Christ crucified, to the Jews a stumbling block and to the Greeks foolishness, but to those who are called, both Jews and Greeks, Christ the power of God and the wisdom of God (1 Corinthians 1:23-24). On this, all free grace people are agreed.

I pray that this book will bring as much joy to your heart as it has to mine.

Earl D. Radmacher, Th.D.
President, Grace Bible Institute
and Seminary of the Northwest

PREFACE

Early in my Christian experience, I was introduced to the controversy over salvation. Shortly after I came to Christ at age 18, I was taught to lead people to Christ by telling them to invite Jesus into their hearts. I practiced that approach for awhile (1958-1960), but in the process of teaching it to others, I saw the fallacy of it and reacted to it. From that moment until now, I have been interested in the subject of salvation.

After I graduated from seminary, I became an itinerant evangelist. During those years, I tried to avoid the controversy because I so detested confrontation. Nevertheless, I had many private discussions about the issue. Except for two occasions when I was asked to do so, I did not speak about it publicly.

For five years, I taught evangelism as an adjunct professor at Dallas Theological Seminary (1974-1979). A popular version of those lectures was later published in a book entitled, *Evangelism: A Biblical Approach* (1984). In that book, I dealt with a number of issues pertaining to salvation including the gospel, faith and repentance. There was also a chapter entitled, "Do not Ask Jesus to Come into Your Heart."

When I was teaching, several students asked me to lecture on Lordship Salvation. I told them I did not have any more room in my course schedule and, besides, at the time, it was not a very well known issue. A group of students prevailed upon me to speak on Lordship Salvation outside of class, which I did. Years later, that lecture was printed in a booklet entitled, *Lordship Salvation: Is it Biblical?* (1983). In it, I examined the requirement for salvation. It is now out-of-print.

When John MacArthur wrote his book *The Gospel According to Jesus*, he referred to the booklet I had written on Lordship Salvation. As a result, I receive so many questions concerning my response, I wrote a paper entitled, "John MacArthur, Jr.'s System of Salvation" (1989). In it, I addressed the issues pertaining to the results of Salvation (it is available free of charge at insightsfromtheword.com).

Since then, I have also written an in-depth study on repentance. "Repentance: The Most Misunderstood Word in the Bible" (2003) is also available free of charge at insightsfromtheword.com.

In other words, this is not the first time I have written on the salvation controversy. There is some overlap between what I have written in the past and what is presented here. Here, however, I expand on what I have written before, mainly, by expounding many of the passages involved. In fact, my purposes here are to clarify the issues and to explain the major passages involved.

I am deeply indebted to others, who have given me insight into some of the passages pertaining to this subject. Their names appear throughout the text. Dr. Radmacher deserves my special thanks for his friendship and encouragement, especially with this project. I am particularly indebted to my brother, John, and to Teresa Rogers, without whose help this project would not have made it to print on time. Last, but by no means least, I am grateful to my wife, who has been a very valuable help.

My only desire is that people clearly understand the gospel of the grace of God and grow in the grace and knowledge of the Lord Jesus Christ. My motivation is pastoral, not polemical.

G. Michael Cocoris
Santa Monica, CA

INTRODUCTION

Since the Protestant Reformation, there has been a salvation controversy between Roman Catholicism and Protestantism. That debate is well known. Roman Catholicism teaches that salvation is by grace through the sacraments and Protestantism insists that salvation is by grace through faith.

There has also been a disagreement among Protestants. Calvinism proclaims predestination and the perseverance of the saints, while Arminianism preaches "free will" and the possibility of genuine believers losing their salvation. The popular expression of this argument is over eternal security. That is an oversimplification of the differences between the two sides, but that issue is involved.

Within the evangelical church in America, there is another controversy concerning the subject of salvation. People in the pew are largely unaware of it. Pastors are more likely to be informed that there is a controversy, but they have probably accepted a viewpoint, which they were taught in the church where they were saved or the seminary they attended—without a carefully examining the details.

This controversy revolves around three aspects of salvation, namely, the *condition* for salvation, the *certainty* of salvation and the *consequences* of salvation. The issues are complex and, therefore, can be confusing. What follows is an attempt to clarify the issues and expound the major passage of Scriptures involved.

The Condition For Salvation

All sides in this controversy agree that salvation is by faith. At the end of a long personal conversation with John MacArthur concerning this controversy, we agreed that the difference between us came down to the definition of faith and the meaning of being a disciple. In fact, he writes, "The lordship controversy is a disagreement over the nature of true faith" (MacArthur, *Faith Works*, hereafter, FW, p. 30).

The disagreement is over the definition of faith and/or how to lead people to Christ. There are three views: True Grace (See 1 Pet. 5:12. a k a "free grace"), Decisionism, sometimes called cheap grace and Lordship Salvation, which is called by some sovereign grace. Decisionism is more of a common practice than a developed doctrine. The Lordship people accuse the True Grace people of Decisionism, a charge they deny. At any rate, there are three positions: True Grace, Decisionism and Lordship Salvation.

True Grace True Grace is the teaching that salvation is by faith alone in Christ alone. The proponents of True Grace point to the Gospel of John and the book of Romans for support of their position.

Decisionism Simply put, Decisionism is the practice of getting people to make a decision in order to be saved. The emphasis is on praying a prayer, usually, asking Jesus to come into your heart. This practice is based on Revelation 3:20, John 1:12 and Romans 10:13.

Lordship Salvation Lordship Salvation is the theological position that in order to be saved, one must turn from sin (or be willing to turn from sin) and make Jesus the Lord of one's life. It rests on an interpretation of such words as repent, believe, Lord and disciple.

The next three chapters will explain each of these views in detail.

Certainity of Salvation

There are two basic views concerning the assurance of salvation.

True Grace According to the True Grace view, assurance is part of faith. Hebrews 11:1 says, "Now faith is the assurance of *things* hoped for, the conviction of things not seen" (Heb. 11:1 NASB), "Now faith is being sure of what we hope for and certain of what we do not see" (Heb. 11:1 NIV). Assurance is based on taking God at His word. The Word of God says, "He who believes in the Son has everlasting life; and he who does not believe the Son shall not see life, but the wrath of God abides on him" (Jn. 3:36 NKJV). What could be clearer? Those who believe have eternal life (Jn. 3:36). God said it. I believe it. That settles it.

Lordship Salvation Lordship Salvation teaches that the basis of assurance is fruit in the life of the believer. Believers are to examine themselves to see if they are in the faith (2 Cor. 13:5). They are to make their calling and election sure (2 Pet. 1:10).

The Consequences of Salvation

True Grace The True Grace position is that at salvation, God changes people (Rom. 6:6-7). God wants His children to stop sinning (Jn. 8:11) and grow to be like Christ (1 Pet. 2:1-2). God desires for His children to produce fruit (Jn. 15:1-11) and good works (Eph. 2:10). God disciplines His children (Heb. 12:6) and rewards those who are faithful unto death (Rev. 2:10). Given what the New Testament says about God working in the believer's life, it is reasonable to assume that the norm is for believers to grow.

In order for believers to grow, however, they must cooperate with God's work in their life. God changes people, but He also tells them they must know, reckon and yield (Rom. 6:3, 11, 13). God lifts and cleanses unproductive branches (Jn. 15:2), but for believers to produce fruit, they must abide in Christ (Jn. 15:4). God disciplines, but He tells His children to endure (Heb. 12:7).

To say that because God does His work in believers, they always grow in grace ignores the commands, as well as the warnings given to them. The commands and warnings of the New Testament are to be taken seriously.

Lordship Salvation Beyond the disagreement over faith, the core of the salvation controversy is the thesis that faith always produces perceivable fruit and that it endures until the end. More specifically, it teaches:

1. God gives repentance and faith to some people (Acts 11:18, 2 Tim. 2:25, Eph. 2:8, 9, Phil. 1:29, Jn. 6:44). God-given faith is real faith.

2. Real faith *always* results in a changed life others can see. As popularly preached, "Salvation is by faith alone, but the faith that saves is not alone." The theological expression is "Justification and sanctification are inseparable. They can be distinguished, but they cannot be divorced." The explanation is that when people are born again, God changes them (Rom. 6:6-7). Believers do not live in sin (1 Jn. 3:6, 9). Simply put, since God changes people, there will be an immediate, *observable* transformation of behavior. People who are born again do not live in sin.

3. Real faith *always* produces *observable* works. Discernable works are the inevitable result of salvation (Jas. 2:14). All believers produce fruit (Jn. 15:2). False faith does not produce works. Faith without works is dead (Jas. 2:17). False faith is a profession without possession. It is head knowledge, not heart knowledge.

4. Real faith endures to the end. Those who endure to the end shall be saved. Genuine believers endure to the end (Mt. 24:13, Jn. 8:31, 1 Jn. 2:19). What God began He will finish (Phil. 1:6). When true believers fall, they get up. Those who do not endure were never saved in the first place.

5. Therefore, since those who genuinely believe are always changed, always produce fruit and always endure to the end, real faith is discernable by looking at a person's life. By their fruit, you shall know them (Mt. 7:16). The test of real faith is fruit. Those who *profess* faith, but who do not produce good works, do not have saving faith. If there is no change in a person's life, we have the right to question if that individual is saved. The New Testament teaches there is a false faith (Lk. 8:13, Jn. 2:23-24, Acts 8:13). If people profess to believe, but do not have changed lives, works and endurance, it is proof that their faith was not saving faith.

6. Everyone should examine their life to see if they are saved. Examine yourself (2 Cor. 13:5). Make your calling and election sure (2 Pet. 1). Therefore, works are the basis of assurance of salvation.

To complicate matters, some who preach True Grace and some who practice Decisionism as the *requirement* for salvation hold to the Lordship Salvation view of the *results* of salvation. They say that salvation is by trusting Christ or by asking Jesus to come into your heart, but they also say that salvation always results in perceivable fruit. Others who hold to True Grace and some who practice Decisionism as the *requirement* of salvation do not believe that salvation always results in immediately observable works. In other words, not all individuals involved in this controversy consistently hold to one of these three positions.

It is even more complicated than that. Some pick and choose various elements from each position. None of the positions are monolithic; that is, not everyone holding to, say, Lordship Salvation, believes the same thing about every issue involved. Not all Lordship defenders agree on the definition of repentance. The same thing is true concerning True Grace "theology." MacArthur distinguishes between one True Grace position he calls, "No-lordship," represented by Ryrie, and another True Grace view he tags as "Radical No-lordship," led by Hodges (MacArthur, FW, pp. 213-218). To say one holds to True Grace or Lordship Salvation does not mean that he or she believes all the things that other True Grace people or Lordship people teach any more than to say a person who is a Democratic or a Republican means that individual believes everything in the Democratic platform or the Republican platform.

Therefore, this is not a debate about individuals. It is not even a dispute over two theologies. This is a controversy over the explanation of a number of terms and passages in the Scripture. What is the definition of faith? What is repentance? What is the meaning of disciple? What is the basis of assurance? Does God give some individuals faith? Are those who come to Christ changed? Do they always produce immediately observable works? Do they always endure to the end?

That is not to say that there is no such thing as a True Grace theology or a Lordship Salvation theology. There is. It is a warning to be careful of hanging a tag on someone and assuming that a particular individual believes everything that goes by that tag. It is also a plea to focus on the text of Scripture and not individuals or even theology.

Summary: The current controversy over salvation within evangelicalism involves three aspects of salvation, namely, the *condition* for salvation, the *certainty* of salvation and the *consequences* of salvation.

So, what does the Scripture say about all of these issues? Which view is Biblical? Of course, all claim their explanation is Biblical. That is why, in the final analysis, a number of passages must be examined.

One other note: if a name appears without a page number, it is usually a reference to a commentator who is commenting on the verse under consideration in his commentary. Virtually all the names with page numbers are authors of books. See the Bibliography.

Part 1

The Condition of Salvation

1
TRUE GRACE

The True Grace view is that salvation is by faith alone in Christ alone. In order to be saved, people must trust Jesus Christ for the gift of eternal life. The Biblical support for the True Grace position is as follows.

The Gospel of John

The only book in the Bible whose purpose is evangelistic is the Gospel of John. The Apostle writes, "And truly Jesus did many other signs in the presence of His disciples, which are not written in this book; but these are written that you may believe that Jesus is the Christ, the Son of God, and that believing you may have life in His name" (Jn. 20:30-31). The Gospel of John was written so that people would believe in Jesus Christ to obtain eternal life. (There are other purposes.)

Throughout his book, John repeatedly says that the requirement for eternal life is to believe. He uses the verb "believe" 100 times. The most famous salvation verse in the Bible says it simply, "For God so loved the world that He gave His only begotten Son, that whoever believes in Him should not perish but have everlasting life" (Jn. 3:16).

What does John mean by "believe?" The Greek verb translated "believe" means, "believe, believe in something, be convinced of something, give credence to, depend on, trust." The Greek noun rendered "faith" means, "faith, trust, confidence" (Arndt and Gingrich; see also Abbott-Smith). In his theology, Erickson speaks of the twofold nature of faith: "giving credence to affirmations and trusting in God" (Erickson, p. 940).

Before one can believe something or trust someone, there must be something to be believed. Hence, the famous theologian, Charles Hodge, says faith includes knowledge (perception of the truth), assent (persuasion of the truth of the object of faith), and trust (reliance) (Hodge on Romans, p. 29).

Knowledge While it is true that the word "believe" does not include knowledge, it is self-evident that faith assumes knowledge. It is impossible for people to believe something they do not know! In the New Testament, hearing precedes believing. "How shall they believe in Him of whom they have not heard?" (Rom. 10:14). "Many of the Corinthians, hearing, believed" (Acts 18:8). People have to hear something before they can believe. Jesus taught that people have to understand something to be saved (Mt. 13:15).

If faith presupposes knowledge, what do people need to know? In the Gospel of John and throughout the New Testament, the knowledge necessary to be saved concerns Jesus Christ. Remember John's purpose statement. He wrote his book that people might "believe that Jesus is the Christ, the Son of God" (Jn. 20:30-31).

What about Jesus Christ needs to be believed? In the Great Commission, Jesus said proclaim the *gospel* (Mk. 16:15, italics added), that is, His death and resurrection (Lk. 24:46-47, 1 Cor. 15:1-8) and those who believed the *gospel* would be saved (Mk. 15:16, italics added). Peter says that the Gentiles heard of the *gospel* and believed (Acts 15:7, italics added). Paul declares, "In Him you also trusted, after you heard the word of truth, the *gospel* of your salvation." (Eph. 1:13, italics added), "For I determined not to know anything among you except Jesus Christ and Him crucified" (1 Cor. 2:2), "O foolish Galatians! Who has bewitched you that you should not obey the truth, before whose eyes Jesus Christ was clearly portrayed among you as crucified?" (Gal. 3:1). According to 1 John, people cannot deny that Jesus is the Christ (1 Jn. 2:22) or that He has come in the flesh (1 Jn, 4:1-3) and be saved.

In *Evangelism: A Biblical Approach*, I wrote, "The object of faith in the New Testament is Jesus Christ. If you were to look up all the occurrences of 'believe' and 'faith' in the New Testament to see what a person must know about Christ, you would discover that a person must believe four things: (1) that Christ is God (John 20:31) and yet (2) a real man (1 John 4:2); (3) that He is the one who died for sins (Rom. 3:25) and (4) rose from the dead (Rom. 10:9)." I concluded, "The object of faith is Jesus Christ, the God-Man, who died and rose. It is not just any 'Christ.' The object of faith must be the Christ who is offered in the gospel, the one revealed in Scripture" (Cocoris, *Evangelism: A Biblical Approach*, p. 74).

Belief To have faith in a person is to believe something about that person. It may be more than that (that is, trust), but it is "certainly not less" (Bromiley in *ISBE*, vol. II, p. 271). It is not necessary to know everything, but it is essential to know and believe something. People cannot "believe" without "belief!"

Again, what is to be believed is that Jesus, the Son of God who became a man, died for sin and arose from the dead, in other words, the gospel (1 Cor. 15:1-5). Hodges states that faith "is not mere assent, or mere trust, it is the intelligent perception, reception, and reliance on the truth, *as revealed in the gospel*!" (Hodges, *Absolutely Free*, hereafter, AF, p. 29, italics added). Bromiley says, "One cannot really trust in Jesus Christ without believing that He is the messiah, the incarnate Son, the crucified and risen Savior" (Bromiley, *ISBE*, vol. II, p. 271).

Pointing out that modern preachers say that faith is not assent to a creed, but confidence in a person, J. Gresham Machen says, "It is impossible to have confidence in a person without assenting to a creed." He goes on to say that faith is more than accepting a creed, but he insists that faith always involves accepting a creed. In his words, "Assent to certain propositions is not the whole of faith, but it is an absolutely necessary element in faith" (Machen, *What is Faith?*, pp. 47-48) and "faith is always based upon knowledge" (Machen, *What is Faith?*, p. 88).

Some wish to debate, "What is the minimum people have to believe in order to be saved?" Should we not be asking, "What is the norm?"

The Gospel of John, the only book in the Bible written to tell people how to obtain eternal life, says people must believe that Jesus is "the Christ, the Son of God" (Jn. 20:31). Does not the expression "the Son of God" include His deity (Jn. 1:1) and humanity (Jn. 1:14)? The term "the Christ" includes His death and resurrection. Jesus Himself taught that (Lk. 24:46)! Early in His ministry, Jesus told Nicodemus that He was the Son of God (Jn. 3:16, 17, 18), who was sent into the world (Jn. 3:13, 3:17), that is, He became a man, who came to die (Jn. 3:14) and would be raised and ascend back to heaven (Jn. 3:13). Jesus told Martha He was the resurrection and the life (Jn. 11:25) and asked her if she believed that (Jn. 11:26). She answered, "I believe that You are the Christ, the Son of God, who is come into the world" (Jn. 11:27). Notice she believed that He was the Son of God, who became a man (cf. "the Son of God, who is come into the world") and that He was the resurrection, which means she believed He would die. You cannot have a resurrection without a death! In the immediate context of John 20:31, the issue is the resurrection of Jesus (20:24-29). Jesus specifically says Thomas believed (Jn. 20:29), meaning he believed in the resurrection of Jesus. Then, John adds, Jesus did "other signs" (the resurrection is a sign!) and the signs are recorded so people would believe that Jesus is the Christ, the Son of God (Jn. 20:31). In the immediate context of the purpose statement of the Gospel of John, believing that Jesus is the Christ includes believing that He arose from the dead. Moreover, *taken as a whole*, the Gospel of John presents Jesus as God (Jn. 1:1), who became a man (Jn. 1:14), who died (Jn. 19:16-18, 30) and who rose from the dead (Jn. 20:1-18, esp. 20:9).

Granted, before the cross not all understood that the Christ would die and be raised from the dead (Mt. 16:16-23, Jn. 20:9), but what was the norm *before* the cross is not necessarily the norm *after* the cross. It is simply undeniable that after the cross, the norm was to preach the gospel, defined as the death and resurrection of Jesus Christ.

After He died and before He ascended, Jesus commissioned the Apostles to preach the gospel (Mk. 16:15). In the context of the

Gospel of Mark, the word "gospel" was used to include Christ's death (cf. Mk. 14:3-9, esp. "this gospel" in Mk. 14:9). Furthermore, in the context of the post-resurrection ministry of Christ, during which time He gave the Apostles the Great Commission, Jesus made it clear that from that point they were to preach His death and resurrection (Lk. 24:46-48).

Peter got the point. In the book of Acts, he preached the death and resurrection of Jesus and that the death and resurrection of Jesus proved He was the Christ! (Acts 2:22-36, esp. 2:36, 3:12-26, esp. 3:18 and 3:26, 4:9, 5:29-32, 10:36-43).

Paul did the same thing. Luke says, "Then Paul, as his custom was, went into them, and for three Sabbaths reasoned with them from the Scriptures, explaining and demonstrating that the Christ had to suffer and rise again from the dead, and *saying,* 'This Jesus whom I preach to you is the Christ'" (Acts 17:2-3). Notice, it was Paul's *custom* to preach the gospel, that is, the death and resurrection of Christ. Paul said to the Corinthians, "It pleased God through the foolishness of the message preached to save those who believe" (1 Cor. 1:21) and he goes on to identify the message when He writes, "But we preach Christ crucified" (1 Cor. 1:23). Paul told the Corinthians that they were saved by believing the gospel, that is, the good news that Jesus died for their sins and rose from the dead (1 Cor. 15:1-5). That means that Paul's message in evangelism included the death and resurrection of Christ. Paul wrote to the Galatians, "O foolish Galatians! Who has bewitched you that you should not obey the truth, before whose eyes Jesus Christ was clearly portrayed among you as crucified?" (Gal. 3:1). In other words, Paul preached Christ crucified to the Galatians when he evangelized them. Paul reminded the Thessalonians that "our gospel did not come to you in word only, but also in power, and in the Holy Spirit and in much assurance" (1 Thess. 1:5). He preached the gospel, the death and resurrection of Christ (1 Cor. 15:1-5), to the Thessalonians.

The issue is not what is the minimum people have to believe in order to be saved. The issue is, "What are we commanded to preach?" The issue is not, "What people understood *before* Christ was crucified?" The issue is, "What are we commanded to preach *after* Christ was crucified?" From the passages on the Great Commission, the preaching of Peter and the practice of Paul, it is plain that we are to preach the death and resurrection of Christ. In the Gospel of John, before Jesus began His ministry, John the Baptist preached, "Behold! The Lamb of God who takes away the sin of the world!" (Jn. 1:29). Certainly, we should point people to the Lamb, who was slain and arose from the dead.

Machen says saving faith may involve a smaller or greater amount of knowledge. The greater the better for the person, but even a small amount of knowledge will do. When Christ, as He is offered to us *in the gospel*, is accepted in faith, the person who believes is saved (Machen, *What is Faith?*, p. 161, italics added).

Trust While one cannot believe without some information and acceptance of that data as true, the faith involved in salvation is more than mental assent to facts. After pointing out that Paul uses the noun (faith) whereas John prefers the verb (believe) with no essential difference in meaning, Bromiley says, "The main sense of the word 'faith' in the NT is that of trust or reliance" (Bromiley, *ISBE*, vol. II, p. 270). Ryrie says, "*Trust* may be particularly appropriate today, for the words *believe* and *faith* sometimes seem to be watered down so that they convey little more than knowing facts" (Ryrie, *So Great Salvation*, hereafter, SGS, p. 121). Some scholars claim that when the verb "believe" is followed by a preposition such as "on" (εισ in Jn. 3:16, επι in Acts 16:31) or "in" (εν in Mark 1:5), it expresses reliance or trust (Bromiley in *ISBE*, vol. II, p. 270, Erickson, p. 940).

At any rate, faith involves both believing *that* and believing *in* (Bruce, p. 12). "The type of faith necessary for salvation involves believing that and believing in or assenting to facts and trusting in a person" (Erickson, p. 940). Berkhof defines saving faith as "as a certain conviction wrought in the heart by the Holy Spirit, as to the truth of the gospel, and a hearty reliance (trust) on the promises of God in Christ" (Berkhof, p. 502).

The Westminster Shorter Catechism says, "Faith in Jesus Christ is the saving grace, whereby we received and rest upon Him alone for salvation, as He is offered to us in the gospel." J. Gretchen Machen says, "Acceptance of the Lord Jesus Christ, as He is offered to us in the gospel of His redeeming work, is saving faith" (Machen, *What is Faith?*, p. 154).

Ryrie says, "To have faith in Christ unto salvation means to have confidence that He can remove the guilt of sin and grant eternal life" (Ryrie, *Basic Theology*, p. 326; see an almost identical statement in *SGS*, p. 119). In his book entitled *So Great Salvation*, he states, "When a person gives credence to the historical facts that Christ died and rose from the dead and the doctoral fact that this was for his sins, he is trusting his eternal destiny to the reliability of those truths" (Ryrie, *SGS*, p. 30). Later in the book, Ryrie says, "The issue is whether or not you believe that His death paid for your sin and by believing in Him you can have forgiveness and eternal life" (Ryrie, *SGS*, p. 119).

Hodges says that faith is "the inward conviction of what God says to us in the gospel is true" (Hodges, AF, p. 31) and, "Saving faith is taking God at His Word in the gospel" (Hodges, *AF*, p. 33). In discussing Martha's confession of faith in John 11, Hodges says, "Thus, by believing the amazing facts about the person of Christ, Martha was *trusting* Him. She was placing her eternal destiny in His hands" (Hodges, AF, p. 39).

Thus faith is believing that Jesus Christ died for my sins and arose from the death and trusting in Him and Him alone to get me to heaven.

What must not be lost sight of, in this controversy, is that salvation is a gift (Rom. 6:23, Jn. 4:10, Eph. 2:8). As Machen says, "Faith means not doing something but receiving something; it means not the earning of a reward but the acceptance of a gift" (Machen, *What is Faith?*, p. 195).

The Roman Road

Of all the books in the New Testament, the book of Romans contains the most detailed discussion of salvation. While there is a lot of "theology" in the first four chapters, a simple outline of salvation is apparent. First, Paul demonstrates that all have sinned (Rom. 1:18-3:20; see also Rom. 3:23). Second, he declares that justification is based on the death of Jesus Christ (Rom. 3:21-31; see also Rom. 5:8). Third, he describes justification by faith (Rom. 4:1-25). Usually with slight variations and sometimes with verses outside Romans, this basic outline has been used to lead people to Christ. Since it follows the flow of Romans, it is popularly called "the Roman Road."

The book of Romans clearly teaches justification by faith. The question is, "How does Romans define faith?" The answer is in Romans chapter 4.

In proving that the doctrine of justification by faith is demonstrated in the Old Testament, Paul points to Abraham in general and Genesis 15:6 in particular (Rom. 4:1-15). In Romans 4:16, he states that Abraham is the father of us all, and later claims that what was written concerning Abraham was written "for us" (Rom. 4:23-24). Thus, Abraham is the Biblical model of faith. What can be learned from Abraham's faith?

Abraham Believed God's Promise In Romans 4:17, Paul quotes the promise God made in Genesis 17:5 and describes Abraham's faith. In other words, *Abraham believed the promise* that God would make him the father of many nations.

Abraham Believed in God's Power Then, Paul describes this God in whom Abraham believed, saying, "who gives life to the dead and calls those things which do not exist as though they did" (Rom. 4:17). God gives life to the dead. This is a reference to Abraham, Sarah and the birth of Isaac (Rom. 4:19). God promised to make Abraham a father of many nations (Gen. 17:5; see Rom. 4:17), which necessitated that Abraham be the father of at least one son, but the body of Abraham and the womb of Sarah his wife were as good as dead from the standpoint of having children. God, however, has the power to give life to such deadness. In other words, God not only *made a promise*, He has the *power to perform what He promised.*

Abraham believed in a God with that kind of power. As Paul put it, "who, contrary to hope, in hope believed, so that he became the father of many nations, according to what was spoken, 'So shall your descendants be'" (Rom. 4:18). Humanly speaking, Abraham was beyond any hope of having a child, but based on the hope he had in God, he *believed God's promise* that his offspring would be as numerous at the stars of the heavens.

Notice, *Abraham believed in God's promise* and *in God's power to perform what He promised.* In order to underscore the nature of Abraham's faith, Paul goes on to state what Abraham did not do.

Abraham Did Not Focus on Human Possibilities Paul says, "And not being weak in faith, he did not consider his own body, already dead (since he was about a hundred years old), and the deadness of Sarah's womb" (Rom. 4:19). Humanly speaking, Abraham, being about a hundred years old, was past child-bearing age. Sarah had not had any children all of her life and now she was past child-bearing age. Abraham did not focus on those facts.

Abraham Did Not Debate Divine Promises Moreover, "He did not waver at the promise of God through unbelief" (Rom. 4:20). The Greek word translated, "waver" means, "to be divided into one's mind, to hesitate." A doubt may have entered his mind, but he did not choose to entertain it to the point of not believing God's promise part of the time, and thus, being divided within himself.

Rather, as Paul says, "(he) was strengthened in faith, giving glory to God, and being fully convinced that what He had promised He was also able to perform" (Rom. 4:20-21). Instead of doubting, debating and being divided, Abraham was *convinced, persuaded and assured that God was able to do what He promised* and he gave glory to God.

Paul concludes, "And therefore 'it was accounted to him for righteousness'" (Rom. 4:22). It was precisely because of such a faith as Paul just described, that God declared Abraham righteous. Abraham *believed God*; he *trusted God's promise.*

Therefore, Abraham's faith was the model of faith. Paul says, "Now it was not written for his sake alone that it was imputed to him, but also for us" (Rom. 4:23-24a). Moses did not write Abraham's story to immortalize Abraham. God had Abraham's faith recorded for others, as an example, the pattern and the model of faith. This is appropriate to Paul's concept of Abraham as the father of all who believe (Rom. 4:16).

How is Abraham's faith a model of faith for us? As Paul explains, "It shall be imputed to us who believe in Him who raised up Jesus our Lord from the dead" (Rom. 4:24b). Righteousness was imputed to Abraham when he had faith, so righteousness is imputed to us when we exercise faith. The parallel that Paul has in mind is more than that. Abraham's faith was a model of faith in that he believed in a God of resurrection. It is when we believe in God who raised Jesus from the dead that we are justified.

As Paul goes on to explain, Jesus "was delivered up because of our offenses, and was raised because of our justification" (Rom. 4:25). Jesus Christ died because we sinned. He arose because by His death our justification has been secured. Faith in Christ is faith in God who has power to resurrect.

To sum it up, the model of faith is Abraham, who believed in the promise and power of God. Faith believes in a God of resurrection power. Faith is taking God at His word (Acts 27:25). If He says He will do something, He has the power to do it and He is faithful to do it.

This passage in Romans 4 is a detailed description of faith. Notice carefully, *faith believes God's promise.* Saving faith believes God's promise that all who trust Jesus Christ, who died for their sins and arose from the dead, will be given eternal life; they will go to heaven. It is taking God at His Word. It is trusting God that He will do what

He said *He* will do. It is believing God's promise, not making God a promise. It is not promising God that you will obey Him for the rest of your life. Those who trust Christ should obey Him, but making a promise to obey God for the rest of one's life is not the requirement for salvation!

Repentance

What about repentance? Traditionally, the True Grace proponents have preached that repentance and faith are required for salvation. While some have concluded that repentance is not a requirement for salvation (Hodges, AF), the New Testament teaches that repentance is required (Lk. 24:47, Acts 17:30, 2 Pet. 3:9).

In *Repentance: The Most Misunderstood Word in the Bible*, I examine every appearance of the verb "repent" and the noun "repentance" in the New Testament. It is available free of charge under Topical Studies at insightsfromtheword.com. Here is an edited version of that study.

What Repentance Is The Greek word translated "repentance" is made up of the two words: "after" and "mind." Thus, the root meaning of the word "repentance" is "afterthought, a change of mind," but the meaning of a word is determined by its usage, not its root. So, how is repentance used in the New Treatment?

In New Testament usage, many passages contain indications in the context that *repentance is a change of mind*. These include Matthew 3:2 (cf. "do not think" in verse 9 with "fruit worthy of repentance" in verse 8), Matthew 9:13 (cf. "trusted in themselves that they were righteous" in Lk. 18:9), Luke 16:30 (cf. "hear" in verse 29 and "persuade" in verse 31), Acts 8:22 (cf. "thought" in verse 20, "heart" in verse 21 and "the thoughts of your heart" in verse 22), Acts 17:30 (cf. "not think" in verse 29 and "ignorance" in verse 30), Acts 26:20 (cf. "repent" versus "do works befitting repentance"), 2 Timothy 2:25 (cf. "know" in verse 25 and "come to their senses" in verse 26), Revelation 2:5 (cf. "repent" between "remember" and "do").

There are Greek authorities who say that the meaning of the Greek word for "repent" in the New Testament is "to change one's mind." For example, one Greek lexicon says that the Greek word translated "repent" means, "to change one's mind or purpose" and "repentance," means, "after-thought" (Abbott-Smith). In his comments on Matthew 3:2, A. T. Robinson, the great Greek scholar, defines "repent" as a "change (think afterwards) [of] their mental attitudes" (See his *Word Pictures in the New Testament*). Julius R. Mantey, who co-authored the famous *A Manual Grammar of the Greek New Testament* (known as "Dana and Mantey") says, "It means to think differently or have a different attitude toward sin and God, etc." (Mantey, p. 193).

There are commentators who agree. In his comments on Luke 3:3, Plummer calls repentance "an inward change of mind." In his commentary on Hebrews 6:1, Westcott says, "It follows, therefore, that 'Repentance *from* dead works' expresses the complete change of mind—of spiritual attitude—which leads the believer to abandon these works and seek some other support for life."

There are theologians who concur. Chafer says, "The word (repentance) means a change of mind" (Chafer, vol. 3, p. 372). Even Erickson, who pours more into the word, admits that "literally" it means, "to think differently about something or have a change of mind" (Erickson, p. 937). Ryrie defines the word "repent" as "to change your mind" (Ryrie, *A Survey of Bible Doctrine*, p. 139).

Simply put, the Greek words for "repent" and "repentance" describe an inward change of thinking or attitude.

What Repentance is Not Repentance is not necessarily a change of mind about sin. Repentance is a change of mind or attitude—period. What people change their mind about is not in or implied by the word. The word repentance is like the word dozen. It does not contain or imply twelve of any one thing. The word dozen simply means twelve, nothing more, and nothing less. A farmer might use the word "dozen" speaking of eggs. A baker may use it to mean twelve donuts. The word "dozen" does not mean twelve eggs or twelve donuts. It simply means "twelve." The context (the farm or the bakery) determines *twelve* what. R. A. Torrey said, "What the repentance, or change of mind, is about must always be determined by the context" (Torrey, p. 355).

In my book *Evangelism: A Biblical Approach*, I point out that in the New Testament, the word repentance has several objects. God is sometimes the object (Acts 20:21). If people have a wrong concept of God, they need to repent, that is, change their mind about God. If they believe that God is an idol, they need to repent and see that the true and living God is the invisible Creator of the universe. Another object of repentance is Christ. In Acts 2, Peter spoke to Jews who had a wrong view of Jesus. They thought of Him as a common criminal. Peter told them to repent (Acts 2: 38), that is, change their minds about Jesus. Still another object of repentance is works (see Heb. 6:1, Rev. 9:20, 16:11, etc.). As a rule, people are of the opinion that works save. People must change their minds about that. Finally, the Scripture speaks about repenting of sin (Rev. 9:21), meaning change ones minds about sin. People need to see that it is serious. It separates them from God (Cocoris, *Evangelism: A Biblical Approach*, pp. 65-72).

In New Testament usage, repentance does not mean to be sorry for sin. Paul plainly demonstrates that sorrow and repentance are two different things. He says, "Your sorrow led to repentance" (2 Cor. 7:9). Sorrow may lead to repentance; sorrow may accompany repentance, but sorrow and repentance are two different things. The New Testament records an illustration of the difference between regretting and repenting. In Acts 2, the Jews regretted what they did to Christ. They were "cut to the heart" and asked, "What shall we do?" (Acts 2:37). It was after their regret that Peter said, "Repent" (Acts 2:38), which shows that regret is different from repentance. It should be pointed out that sorrow does not have to precede repentance. Paul says the goodness of God can also lead to repentance

(Rom. 2:4). D. L. Moody said the sinner is not to seek sorrow, but the Savior. By the way, if repentance is being sorry for sin, how much sorrow is enough?

In New Testament usage, repentance is not turning from sin. The New Testament makes a distinction between repentance and turning. There is another Greek word for turning and it is never translated "repent." In addition, Acts 26:20 clearly demonstrates that repenting and turning are two different things. Paul says that the Gentiles should "repent and turn to God" (literal translation). Furthermore, the New Testament speaks about repenting and bringing forth fruit fit for repentance (Lk. 3:8, Acts 26:20), which indicate that repenting is different than turning from sin.

The conclusive evidence that repentance does not mean to be sorry for sin or to turn from sin is that in the Old Testament, God repents! To illustrate, in the King James Version of the Old Testament, the word repent occurs forty-six times. Thirty-seven of these times, God is the one repenting (or not repenting). If repentance means sorrow for sin or turning from sin, God is a sinner.

The Relationship to Faith In many passages, faith is the one and only requirement for salvation (Gen. 15:6, Jn. 3:16, Acts 16:31). Not only does the Bible repeatedly mention faith as the single requirement, in critical places, it does not mention repentance. The Gospel of John is the only book in the Bible that has as it purpose to bring people to Christ (Jn. 20:31). Yet the Gospel of John does not mention the words "repent" or "repentance" one single time. The most detailed book in the Bible on salvation is the book of Romans. The chapter in Romans on what one must do to be saved is Romans 4, but Romans 4 does not contain the words "repent" or "repentance." In fact, the word "repentance" only occurs once in the book of Romans (Rom. 2:14) and there it is a virtual synonym for faith. The only book in the Bible written to defend the gospel is Galatians. Neither the word "repent" nor the word "repentance" makes an appearance in that book at all.

On the other hand, some passages say that repentance is required (Lk. 24:47, Acts 2:38, 3:19, 5:31, 17:30, 26:20, 2 Pet. 3:9, Rev.

9:20-21, 16:9, 11) and in these verses there is no mention of faith. To complicate matters, faith and repentance appear together in three places (Mk. 1:16, Acts 20:21, Heb. 6:1). The absence of repentance in critical passages on salvation and yet the insistence on repentance in others is a problem. What is the relationship between faith and repentance? Virtually all conclude that repentance and faith are inseparable.

John Calvin says, "Can true repentance exist without faith? By no means. But although they cannot be separated, they ought to be distinguished" (Calvin, *Institutes of the Christian Religion*, 3, 3, 5). In other words, repentance is "the whole work of turning to God, of which not the least important part is faith" (Calvin, 3, 3, 5). Berkhof states, "True repentance never exists except in conjunction with faith, while, on the other hand, wherever there is true faith, there is also real repentance. . . . The two cannot be separated; they are simply complementary parts of the same process" (Berkhof, p. 487). Erickson agrees, "As we examine repentance and faith, it should be remembered that they cannot really be separated from one another" (Erickson, p. 935). Chafer concludes, "It (repentance) is included in believing and could not be separated from it" (Chafer, vol. 3, p. 373). In a sermon entitled "Faith and Repentance Inseparable" Charles Haddon Spurgeon put it like this: "The repentance which is here commanded is the result of faith; it is born at the same time with faith—they are twins, and to say which is the elder-born passes my knowledge. It is a great mystery; faith is before repentance in some of its acts, and repentance before faith in another view of it; the fact being that they come into the soul together."

In *Repentance: The Most Misunderstood Word in the Bible*, I conclude, "The message of repentance to unbelievers is that they have to change their minds. Depending on their mindset, they needed a shift in thinking about their merit to enter the world to come, their righteousness, their works, the nature of God and who Jesus Christ is. In other words, repentance is changing one's mind from trusting one's merit, righteousness, works or idols to trusting Jesus Christ. Repentance, then, if not equivalent to faith in Christ, is conceptually equivalent to faith or essentially synonymous with faith."

There are places in the New Testament where repentance is a virtual synonym for faith. Jesus said that the men of Nineveh *repented* at the preaching of Jonah (Mt. 12:41); the book of Jonah says that the people of Nineveh *believed* God (Jonah 3:5). Peter told the people in Cornelius's house that "whoever believes in Him will receive remission of sins" (Acts 10:43) and when Peter got back to Jerusalem, he said that "God gave them the same gift as *He gave* us when we believed on the Lord Jesus Christ" (Acts 11:17), but the people in Jerusalem said, "Then God has also granted to the Gentiles repentance to life" (Acts 11:18). What has been described as faith (Acts 10:43, 11:17) is now called repentance (Acts 11:18). Paul declared to the people of Athens that God "commands all men everywhere to repent" (Acts 17:29-30), but the episode ends with Luke saying that some "believed" (Acts 17:34).

Summary: The New Testament teaches that salvation is by faith alone in Christ alone; that is, people must trust Jesus Christ, who died for their sins and arose from the dead, to get them to heaven.

Faith is believing God's promise. It is trusting Jesus Christ for the gift of eternal life. Realizing that I am a sinner and that I cannot save myself, I *believe* that Jesus Christ paid for my sin and I *trust* Him and Him alone for the forgiveness of my sins and the gift of eternal life. Paul says he was a "pattern to those who are going to *believe on* Him *for* everlasting life" (1 Tim. 1:16, italics added). Faith is *trusting* Jesus Christ *for* everlasting life. It is trusting Jesus Christ to get me to heaven.

Years ago, a UCLA student told me that he attended a church, which taught Lordship Salvation. He believed it and proclaimed it. Then, he saw the fallacy of it. When I asked him what changed his mind, he said, "Romans 3:24 says, 'We are justified freely.' 'Freely' means, 'without payment.' It cost the Father His Son. It cost the Son

His life. The only one to whom it was free, without payment, is the one who believes." That young man made a very valid point. The Greek word translated "freely" in Romans 3:24 is translated "without cost" in Revelation 22:17 (NASV).

As Ryrie says, grace is costly to the donor, but free to the recipient (Ryrie, SGS, p. 17). Salvation is absolutely free. It is without cost to those who will trust Christ for the gift of eternal life.

2
DECISIONISM

Decisionism is the practice of getting people to pray a prayer in order to be saved. The prayer can be something as simple as, "Lord, save me." Much more common is the practice of telling people to "Ask Jesus to come into your heart."

The feeling is that if people asked Jesus into their heart, they are saved. Believers tell people to pray that prayer and after that prayer is finished, believers ask, "Do you know for sure that you are saved? If the person who prayed the prayer says, "No," believers declare, "If you ask Jesus to come into your heart, you are saved, because, Jesus said if you asked, He would come in and Jesus is not a liar." In a sense, sinners are being told to make a decision and have faith in that decision! Three verses are often used to maintain Decisionism.

Revelation 3:20

Jesus told the church at Laodicea, "Behold, I stand at the door and knock. If anyone hears My voice and opens the door, I will come in to him and dine with him, and he with Me" (Rev. 3:20). This verse is the foundation of the practice of telling sinners to ask Jesus into their heart in order to be saved, but this verse is not speaking about salvation.

The Context Revelation 3:20 is in a letter addressed to a church in Laodicea. Granted, the people are half-hearted, self-sufficient, and deceived about their spiritual need, but they are believers. The crowning indication is the Lord tells them He will chasten them (Rev.

3:19). The Greek word translated "chasten" means, "to train a child, chasten, correct," which is the activity of God to believers (Heb. 12:5-8, especially 12:8).

The Verse Revelation 3:20 pictures Jesus knocking at the door of the *church*. If any individual will invite Him in, that person will have fellowship with the Lord. Notice carefully, the text says that Jesus will come "in to" (two different words), not come "into" (one word). The verse is saying that Jesus will come *in* the church *to* the person, not that Jesus will come *into* the person. When He gets in the church with the person, they will dine together, a picture of fellowship.

The point of Revelation 3:20 is that lukewarm, self-sufficient, spiritually deceived believers have pushed God aside; they needed fellowship. It is not teaching that a person is saved by asking Jesus into his or her heart. It is not even talking about salvation!

John 1:12

John 1:12 says, "But as many as received Him, to them He gave the right to become children of God, to those who believe in His name" (Jn. 1:12). Those who practice Decisionism say this verse teaches that salvation is receiving Jesus into your heart, so if you ask Him to come in, He will come in and you will be saved. John 1:12 is not talking about receiving Jesus into your heart.

The Context John writes, "He was in the world, and the world was made through Him, and the world did not know Him" (Jn. 1:10). The point here is simply that Jesus came into the world He made and the world did not know Him, that is, they did not recognize Him.

John continues, "He came to His own and His own did not receive Him" (Jn. 1:11). In the Greek text, the first occurrence of the phrase "His own" is neuter, that is, He came to His own place, and the second is masculine, that is, He came to His own people, the Jews. The Jews did not receive Him. The Greek world translated "receive" means, "to receive, accept, receive kindly or hospitably" (A-S).

It carries the connotation of "welcome." The world did not recognize Him (Jn. 1:10); His own people did not welcome Him (Jn. 1:11). Instead of a welcome mat, He received a door slammed in His face. Those whose whole history had been a training to receive Him, instead rejected Him.

The Verse John moves from the world (Jn. 1:10) to the nation of Israel (Jn. 1:11) to individuals (Jn. 1:12). Whereas the world did not recognize Him and the Jews did not welcome Him, individuals who do so are given a great promise. John says, "But as many as received Him, to them He gave the right to become children of God, to those who believe in His name" (Jn. 1:12). The point is that in contrast to the world who did not recognize Him (1:10) and Israel who rejected Him (1:11), individuals, who receive Him, that is, recognize and welcome Him, are given the right to become children of God.

Seen in context, it is obvious that John 1:12 has nothing to do with a subjective receiving of Jesus into a person's heart. Receiving is the objective recognizing and welcoming Him. Furthermore, John explains what he means by "receive Him" when he adds, "to those who believe in His name." According to the verse itself, the way to receive Him is to believe in His name, not ask Him to come into one's heart.

Commentators concur. Godet, who wrote one of the classic commentaries on John, put it like this: "The figurative, and consequently, somewhat vague, term *receive*, required to be explained, precisely defined; for the readers must know accurately the means by which they may place themselves among the number of 'all those who.' Hence the apprehended phrase ... 'to those who believe on His name.'" Alford, the famous Greek exegete, says that "receive" here means, "recognized Him as that which He was—the Word of God and Light of men." Westcott says the national rejection is qualified by the personal belief of some. He adds that the reception of Christ is explained as faith. Plummer says receive "denotes the spontaneous acceptance of the Messiah."

In other words, John 1:12 is not teaching that sinners are to ask Jesus to come into their hearts. It is saying people should accept Christ for who He is and that acceptance is trusting Him.

Romans 10:13

Paul says, "For whoever calls on the name of the LORD shall be saved" (Rom. 10:13). The question is, "What is the content of the calling?" Or, "What is said when one calls on the name of the Lord?" There is nothing in this verse or this passage that even remotely implies that the calling involves asking Jesus into your heart. Such a suggestion can only be found by importing it into the passage. It certainly does not come from the passage.

Summary: The New Testament does not teach Decisionism. The verses used to teach that people are saved by asking Jesus into their heart do not teach such a notion.

Several things need clarification. People have been saved when Revelation 3:20 was used, but that was in spite of the verse and not because of it. On the other hand, people have been deceived by this approach. Because they were told that praying a prayer was the *means* of salvation, they thought they were saved.

Faith is the *means* of salvation. The indwelling of Christ is the *result*. There are other results of salvation, for example, the sealing of the Holy Spirit. It is no more proper to make His indwelling (that is, asking Jesus to come into your heart) the means, than it is to make sealing the means. If you told someone to pray to ask God to seal her with the Spirit, and the person did, would that person be saved? My personal opinion is that we cannot really say one way or the other. It depends on whether or not that individual understood the gospel and trusted Christ. We must be Biblical, and the Biblical word for what a person must do to be saved is "believe." How much better it would be to point people to Christ and the cross and exhort them to trust Him and His finished work.

In leading a person to Christ, there is nothing wrong with having an individual pray. Jesus said to the woman at the well, "If you knew the gift of God, and who it is who says to you, 'Give Me a drink,' you would have asked Him, and He would have given you living water" (Jn. 4:10). Praying a prayer is not the problem. The problem is that it is possible to pray a prayer and not actually get saved! So we must be crystal clear about what people must do to be saved.

For a more detailed discussion of these verses, especially Revelation 3:20, see the chapter "Don't Ask Jesus to Come into Your Heart" in *Evangelism: A Biblical Approach* by G. Michael Cocoris. It is available at insightsfromtheword.com.

3
LORDSHIP SALVATION

Lordship salvation is the theological position that in order to be saved people must make Jesus Christ the Lord of their lives. A number of different arguments are used to arrive at such a conclusion. Years ago, I wrote a booklet on Lordship Salvation entitled *Lordship Salvation: Is it Biblical?* (It is now out-of-print.) In it, I said there were five arguments used to prove Lordship Salvation. Here is an edited version of that material.

Repentance

The Lordship View The first argument used to prove Lordship Salvation is the word repentance. Not all proponents of Lordship Salvation define "repentance" the same way. Some define repentance as being willing to turn from sin. Erickson says, "Repentance is godly sorrow for one's sin together with a resolution to turn from it" (Erickson, p. 937). Others, however, go further saying it is actually turning from sin. Berkhof defines repentance as a "change wrought in the conscious life of the sinner, by which he turns away from sin" (Berkhof, p. 486). MacArthur admits that "literally" repentance means "afterthought" or "change of mind," but he goes on to say that "biblically its meaning does not stop there . . . it *always* speaks of a change of purpose and specifically a turning from sin" (MacArthur, FW, p. 162). Repentance has been described as "forsaking of sin, and turning from it" (*Barnes Notes* on Rom. 2:4). Stott says, "True, *metanoia* [Greek 'repentance'] means literally 'a change of mind,' but it describes such a change of mind as involves a change of attitude, direction and behavior" (Stott, pp. 15, 17). Notice, these various definitions include feeling sorrow for sin, turning from sin, forsaking sin and a change of behavior.

The Meaning of Repentance There is simply no question about the fact that the Bible teaches that one must repent in order to be saved (Acts 17:30, 2 Peter 3:9). The question is, "What is the meaning of repentance?" Does it mean to feel sorrow for sin? Does it mean to turn from sin, that is, to change your conduct? The answer is, "No."

As has been point out, the Greek words translated "repent" and "repentance" are used in the New Treatment of a change of mind. These words do not mean to have *sorrow for sin*. The New Testament makes a distinction between repentance and remorse. There is another Greek word for regret. It appears five times in the New Testament (Mt. 21:29, 32, 27:3, 2 Cor. 7:8, Heb. 7:21). It describes "sorrow for something done and wishing it undone," but "forgiveness of sins is nowhere promised" for it (Trench, p. 258). Judas was "remorseful" (Mt. 27:3), but he did not get saved. On the other hand, the Greek word for repentance "does not properly signify sorrow for having done amiss" (Trench, p. 257). By the way, Esau shed tears, but that did not change anything (Heb. 12:16-17).

In the New Testament, repentance is not *turning from sin*. There is another Greek word for turning and it is never translated "to repent." Moreover the Greek word that is translated "repent" in the New Testament is used of changing one's mind *to sin*! "Plutarch tells of two murderers, who having spared a child, afterwards 'repented' and sought to slay it" (Trench, p. 258).

Remember, the conclusive proof that repentance does not mean to be sorry for sin or to turn from sin is that in the Old Testament, God repents! See the chapter entitled, "True Grace," for a more detailed examination of repentance.

Faith

The Lordship View The second argument used to support Lordship Salvation is the use of the word "faith." The adherents to Lordship Salvation pour such concepts as commitment, making Christ the Lord and even obedience into the word "faith"! From the word "commitment," the conclusion is that people must give their lives to Christ.

John R. Stott says, "Faith is commitment" and faith is "a complete commitment" (Stott, p. 17). Enlow states, "To 'believe on the Lord Jesus Christ' involves more than knowledge, assent, and trust (reliance). True, one must know about God's provision, he must assent to the truth of the gospel and he must rely on Christ to save him, but to believe on the Lord Jesus Christ means more than to believe that He is Lord and more than to rely on Him to give eternal life. It means to receive Christ as one's own Lord, the ruler of one's own life" (Enlow, p. 3). MacArthur writes, "Faith encompasses obedience" (MacArthur, *The Gospel According to Jesus*, hereafter GAJ, p. 173), "Clearly the biblical concept of faith is inseparable from obedience" (MacArthur, GAJ, p. 174), "Faith encompasses obedience" and "faith is not complete unless it is obedient" (MacArthur, GAJ, p. 173, FW, p. 50). Stott also argues that obedience is an element of faith. According to him, the expression, "obedience of faith," in Romans 1:5 means, "obedience which is faith" (Stott, p. 17).

The Meaning of Faith Obviously, the New Testament teaches that faith is the means of salvation (Jn. 3:16, Eph. 2:8). The question is, "What is the meaning of faith?" The Greek verb translated "believe" means, "believe, believe in something, be convinced of something, give credence to, depend on, trust" and the noun rendered "faith" means, "faith, trust, confidence" (Arndt and Gingrich; see also Abbott-Smith).

After a detailed discussion of the meaning of the Greek word, Charles Hodge, the famous Princeton theologian, concludes: "That faith, therefore, which is connected with salvation, includes knowledge, that is, a perception of the truth and its qualities; assent, or the persuasion of the truth of the object of faith; and trust, or reliance. The exercise, or state of mind expressed by the word *faith,* as used in the Scriptures, is not mere assent, or mere trust, it is the intelligent perception, reception, and reliance on the truth, as revealed in the gospel!" (Hodge, p. 29).

The phrase "obedience of faith" means that faith is an act of obedience to the command of God as given in the gospel. Refusal to trust Christ is an act of disobedience. Murray says "obedience of faith" means "obedience which consists of faith." In other words, we are to obey the command to believe.

The synonyms for "faith" in the New Testament cannot mean "commit." For example, in John 4:4 Jesus said, "But whosoever drinks of the water that I shall give him shall never thirst." Later, Jesus said, "Whoso eats my flesh and drinks my blood, has eternal life" (Jn. 6:54). Obviously, these statements suggest "appropriation," not commitment. The same thing is true of the idea of 'looking' implied by John 3:14-15 (cf. Num. 21:6-9). Hogan has written, "In 'looking' there is no idea of committal of life, no thought of healing being deserved, no question concerning the subsequent life of the looker, no possibility of surrender to the object of vision" (Hogan, p. 16).

Faith is required for salvation; but faith, in the New Testament sense of the term, is believing that Jesus Christ is the Son of God and that He died and rose from the dead (Jn. 20:31, Rom. 4:25, 10:9). It is trusting in Him for eternal life. It is not the commitment of one's entire life to Him. In order to be saved, sinners do not give their lives to Christ. That is backwards. Christ gave His life for sinners and all sinners can do is trust the One who died for them.

See the chapter above entitled "True Grace" for a more detailed examination of faith in the New Testament.

Lord

The Lordship View A third argument, sometimes used to support the Lordship position, is the use of the word "Lord." According to the Lordship theology, the word "Lord" (the Greek word *kurios*) means, "master." Therefore, in order to be saved we must submit to Christ as Master.

Stott says, "Why does Paul tell the Philippian jailer that he must believe in 'the Lord Jesus Christ' to be saved if he must only believe in Him as Savior (16:31, cf. 11:17)? And why does Peter, when announcing to Cornelius the good news of peace through Jesus Christ, immediately add in a parenthesis, 'He is Lord of all' (10:36)? To confess Jesus as Lord, which in Romans 10:9 is so clearly made a condition of salvation, means more than 'subscribing to the gospel announcement that a living Lord attests an efficacious death.' It *is* that. It is also an acknowledgement of the deity of Jesus. But it implies as much that Jesus is 'my Lord' as that He is 'the Lord.' It was in comparison with 'the excellency of the knowledge of Christ Jesus my Lord' that St. Paul counted everything else but loss (Philippians 3:8)" (Stott, p. 18).

MacArthur concurs, "Certainly the word *Lord* means deity wherever Scripture calls Jesus 'Lord' in connection with the gospel message. That Christ is God is a fundamental component of the gospel message. No one who denies the deity of Christ can be saved (1 John 4:2, 3)" (MacArthur, GAJ, p. 208). Then he says, "But inherent in the idea of deity is authority, dominion and the right to command" (MacArthur, GAJ, p. 208). Insisting that Lordship "includes the ideas of dominion, authority, sovereignty and the right to govern," MacArthur contends that implicit in the phrase "confess ... Jesus as Lord" in Romans 10:9 is the idea that "people who come to Christ for salvation must do so in obedience to Him, that is, with a willingness to surrender to Him as Lord" (MacArthur, GAJ, p. 207).

The Meaning of Lord The word "Lord" in the New Testament has a variety of meanings including "sir," "owner," "master," and "God." When used of Christ, it often means "God." The reason for this, and the proof of this, is simple. In the Old Testament, the Jews did not pronounce the personal name of God. Instead, they said "Lord." In the Septuagint, the Greek translation of the Old Testament, the term "Lord" was used for God's name; thus, the word "Lord" meant "God." By calling Jesus Christ "the Lord Jesus Christ," the New Testament is attributing deity to Him.

Westcott writes, "To 'confess Jesus,' which in the connection can only mean to confess 'Jesus as Lord' (I Cor. xii.3, Rom. x.9), is to recognize divine sovereignty in One Who is truly man, or, in other words, to recognize the union of the divine and human in one Person, a truth which finds its only adequate expression in the fact of the Incarnation" (Westcott, *The Epistles of John*, p. 142).

B. B. Warfield agrees that the word "Lord" is a reference to deity. He writes, "The full height of this reverence may be suggested to us by certain passages in which the term 'Lord' occurs in citations from the Old Testament, where its reference is to Jehovah, though in the citations it seems to be applied to Jesus. Like the other Synoptists, Luke cites, for instance, from Isaiah the promise of a voice crying in the wilderness, 'Make ye ready the way of the Lord, make His paths straight' (Isaiah 3:4), and applies it to the coming of John the Baptist whom he represents as preparing the way for Jesus' manifestation. As in the case of the other evangelists, the inference lies close that by 'the Lord' here Luke means Jesus, whose coming he thus identifies with the advent of Jehovah and whose person he seems to identify with Jehovah. On the other hand, in passages like Luke 1:17, 76, although the language is similar, it seems more natural to understand the term 'Lord' as referring to God Himself, and to conceive the speaker to be thinking of the coming of Jehovah to redemption in Jesus without necessary identification of the person of Jesus with Jehovah. The mere circumstance, however, that the reader is led to pause over such passages and to consider whether they may not intend by their 'Lord'—who is Jehovah—to identify the person of Jesus with Jehovah, is significant. We should never lose from sight the outstanding fact that to men familiar with the LXX and the usage of 'Lord' as the personal name of the Deity there illustrated, the term 'Lord' was charged with associations of deity, so that a habit of speaking of Jesus as 'the Lord,' by way of eminence, such as is illustrated by Luke and certainly was current from the beginning of the Christian proclamation (Luke 19:31), was apt to carry with it implications of deity, which, if not rebuked or in some way guarded against, must be considered as receiving the sanction of Jesus Himself" (Warfield, pp. 105-106).

J. Gresham Machen, in reference to the widespread pagan use of the term "Lord," observes, "When the early Christian missionaries, therefore, called Jesus 'Lord,' it was perfectly plain to their pagan hearers everywhere that they meant to ascribe divinity to Him and desired to worship Him" (Machen, *What is Faith?*, p. 306).

More recently, Hans Bietenhard, in *The New International Dictionary of New Testament Theology,* writes, "In accordance with the usage of the Hellenistic synagogues God is frequently called *kurios* [Greek 'Lord'], especially in the numerous quotations from the Old Testament in which *kurios* stands for Yahweh, corresponding to the custom of pronouncing the title *kurios* instead of the tetragrammaton in public reading... *kurios* frequently denotes God in the Lucan birth narratives" (Bietenhard, *NIDNT,* vol. 2. p. 513).

At the end of the article on "Lord" by Bietenhard, the general editor, Colin Brown, adds that "Wilhelm Bousset . . . argued that the application of the title *kurios* to Christ originated with the Gentile church. . . and that this direct transferal of this holy name of the almighty God was actually almost a deification of Jesus." He notes further that "a similar position was adopted by R. Bultmann" (Brown, *NIDNT*, vol. 2. p. 515).

The point is that the New Testament is claiming that Jesus Christ is Lord, that is, that He is God. As the God-man, He is our Savior. The word "Lord" in the phrase, "Believe in the Lord Jesus Christ," is no different than, "Believe President Bush will do it." The term "President" is his title. It indicates his position and his ability to follow through on promises. As Hodges points out, this obviously is not the same thing as saying, "Submit to the authority of President Bush" (Hodges, AF, p. 170). In a similar fashion, the term "Lord," when used of Jesus Christ, indicates His position as God and thus His ability to save and grant eternal life.

The Greek word translated "Lord" in the title, the Lord Jesus Christ, is *kurios*. Had the New Testament intended to convey that an individual had to make Jesus Christ master of one's life in order to be saved, it would have used another Greek word, namely, the Greek word *despotes*, from which we get our word despot. It means "master." It is used in the New Testament, but only rarely (for example, 2 Pet. 2:1). It is not the word used in the title, "The Lord Jesus Christ." There is a verb form of *kurios* (*kurieuo*) and there is a verb form of *despotes* (*despotas*). If the New Testament had intended to communicate that we must make Christ Lord, why did it not say so with the Greek words available?

Also, using the method that says "Lord" in the command, "Believe on the Lord Jesus Christ" means, making Christ master, someone could say, the meaning of "Christ" is He is the future King in the kingdom. Therefore, in order to be saved, people must believe that Jesus is the future King, who will reign on the earth (see Ryrie, SGS, p. 106).

Disciple

The Lordship View A fourth argument used for Lordship Salvation is that the concept of discipleship supports the Lordship position for salvation. Discipleship demands all. Therefore, in order to be saved, we must give all to Christ.

In his book, *Evangelism and the Sovereignty of God,* J. I. Packer argues, "More than once, Christ deliberately called attention to the radical break with the past that repentance involves. 'If any man will come after me, let him deny himself, and take up his cross daily, and follow me ... *whosoever* will lose his life for my sake, the same (but only he) shall save it.' 'If any man come to me, and hate not his father, and mother, and wife, and children, and brethren, and sisters, yea, and his own life also (i.e., put them all decisively second in his esteem), he cannot be my disciple... *whoever* he be of you that forsaketh not all that he hath, he cannot be my disciple.' The repentance that Christ requires of His people consists in a settled refusal to set any limit to the claims which He may make on their lives. Our Lord knew — who better? — how costly His followers would find it to maintain this refusal, and let Him *have* His way with them all the time, and therefore He wished them to face out and think through the implications of discipleship before committing *themselves.* He did not desire to make disciples under false pretenses. He had no interest in gathering vast crowds of professed adherents who would melt away as soon as they found out what following Him actually demanded of them. In our own presentation of Christ's gospel, therefore, we need to lay a similar stress on the cost of following Christ, and make sinners face it soberly before we urge them to respond to the message of free forgiveness. In common honesty, we must not conceal the fact that free forgiveness in one sense will cost everything; or else our evangelizing becomes a sort of confidence trick. And where there is no clear knowledge, and hence no realistic recognition of the real claims that Christ makes, there can be no repentance, and therefore no salvation" (Packer, pp. 72-73).

MacArthur's thesis is that "every Christian is a disciple" (MacArthur, GAJ, p. 196). Any distinction between believer and disciple is "purely artificial" (MacArthur, GAJ, page 196) and a call to Christian discipleship explicitly demands "total dedication. It is full commitment with nothing knowingly or deliberately held back" (MacArthur, GAJ, p. 197).

The Meaning of Discipleship Granted, discipleship demands all, but in the New Testament, justification (sonship) and discipleship are two different things.

It ought to be transparently obvious that there is a difference between being a believer and being a disciple. The moment people trust Christ, they are given the gift of eternal life (Jn. 4:10, Rom. 6:23). They are justified "freely" (Rom. 3:24), "without cost" (Rev. 22:17 NASV). On the other hand, to be a disciple costs (Lk. 14:28). This is not a paradox; it is a simple statement of fact.

The Greek word translated "disciple" means, "learner, pupil." When used to designate a learner of Christ, it has a variety of meanings. In a sense, its meaning evolves. At first, it is used in a general sense of anyone who learns from Christ (Mt. 8:21, Lk. 16:17, Jn. 4:1). Apparently, some of these disciples were not even saved (Jn. 6:60-66). All of these learned from Christ, but they did not travel with Him. Disciple is also used specifically of the twelve apostles who forsook their occupations and traveled with Christ (Mt. 4:18-20, Mt. 10:1, etc.). Thus, in the gospels, a disciple was anyone from a learner who did not trust Christ to a constant companion who traveled with Him. Some obviously did not learn very much. Therefore, Christ had to define a true learner, that is, a genuine disciple.

To learn, people must do more than call themselves students and listen to a teacher. There is a vast difference between enrolling in a class and actually learning. In the case of learning from Christ, one must begin by trusting in Him (Jn. 8:30), but simply trusting Christ for eternal life does not guarantee that the person will learn from Him. Thus, "Jesus said to those Jews who believed in Him, 'If you abide in My word, you are My disciples indeed'" (Jn. 8:31). The word translated "indeed" means "truly." The true disciple is not only one who has trusted Christ (Jn. 8:30), but one who also commences to obey Christ (Jn. 8:31). In other words, Jesus told those who believed, and who therefore had eternal life, "Now if you really want to *learn*, you must continue in My word, that is, obey Me." Thus, there is a difference between being "a believer" and being "a disciple."

Peter believed that Jesus was the Messiah (Jn. 1:41-42 and Jn. 2:11) before he became a disciple (Mt. 4:18-20).

If discipleship is tantamount to salvation, one must be baptized in order to be saved. Matthew 28:19, 20 says, "Go ye therefore and teach all nations, baptizing them in the name of the Father and of the Son and of the Holy Spirit, teaching them to observe all things whatsoever I have commanded you; and, I am with you always, even unto the end of the age. Amen." In the Greek text, "make disciples" is an imperative and the only imperative in the last paragraph of Matthew's Gospel. Clustered around the command to "make disciples" are three participles: going, baptizing and teaching. Going includes introducing people to Christ (cf. Mk. 16:15-16). Baptizing identifies a believer with the body of believers, like a wedding band identifies the wearer as married. Teaching, of course, is instruction. The discipling process, then, involves introduction to the person of Christ, identification with the body of Christ and instruction in the commands of Christ. To say the same thing another way, in order for a person to be a disciple, he or she must trust Christ, be baptized, and begin to obey His commandments. If being a disciple is the same thing as being a believer, one must be baptized and obey the commands of Christ in order to go to heaven.

The Rich Young Ruler

The Lordship View Another argument used for Lordship Salvation is taken from the conversation between Jesus and the rich young ruler. When asked what he had to do to inherit eternal life, Jesus told the rich young ruler to sell all that he had and give it to the poor. In other words, Jesus demanded all. Therefore, in order to be saved people must give Christ control over all of their lives.

In his commentary on the Gospel of Mark, Swete says, "The sale and distribution of his property were the necessary preparations in his case for the complete discipleship which admits to the Divine kingdom" (Swete, p. 226). MacArthur's analysis of this story is that Christ "gave a message of works and at this point did not even mention faith or the facts of redemption" (MacArthur, GAJ, p. 79), "our Lord revealed nothing of Himself or the facts of the gospel. He did not invite the man to believe" (MacArthur, GAJ, p. 83). According to MacArthur, the issue in the story is "will this man obey the Lord?... Christ was saying 'Are you going to do what I want you to do. Who will run your life, you or I?'... He was telling the young man 'unless I can be the highest authority in your life, there is no salvation for you'" (MacArthur, GAJ, pp. 86-87).

This does not mean, MacArthur assures us, that a person must literally give away everything he owns to become a Christian, but a person does have to be willing to forsake all. "Jesus' request of this man was simply meant to establish whether he was willing to submit to the sovereignty of Jesus over his life" (MacArthur, p. GAJ, 87). MacArthur hastens to add that he believes salvation is by grace through faith, "but people with genuine faith do not refuse to acknowledge their sinfulness. They sense that they have offended the holiness of God and do not reject the lordship of Christ... saving faith is a commitment to leave sin and follow Jesus Christ at all costs. Jesus takes no one unwilling to come on those terms (MacArthur, GAJ, p. 87)... there must be a *willingness* to obey" (MacArthur, GAJ, p. 88).

The Meaning of the Rich Young Ruler Conversation The answer Jesus gave to the rich, young ruler is often seriously misunderstood. In the first place, Jesus inquired of him, "Why do you call Me good? No one *is* good but One, *that is,* God" (Mk. 10:18). In other words, Jesus asked him, "Are you recognizing that I am God?" The young man did not answer.

Having tried the God-ward approach, Christ turned to the man-ward approach. He says, "You know the commandments" (Mk. 10:19). Notice that He did not say, "Go do the commandments." He simply said, "You *know* the commandments" and quoted the last six of the Ten Commandments, the ones that refer to man's relationship to man. Why did the Lord bring up the Ten Commandments? The answer is that He was using the Law lawfully. Paul explains in 1 Timothy 1:8, 9, "that the law *is* good if one uses it lawfully, knowing this: that the law is not made for a righteous person, but for *the* lawless and insubordinate, for *the* ungodly and for sinners, for *the* unholy and profane, for murderers of fathers and murderers of mothers, for manslayers" (1 Tim. 1:8-9). Thus, the Lord is using the Law lawfully in that He is using it to teach the young man that he is a sinner, and needs a Savior.

When the young man says, "All these things I have kept from my youth" (Mk. 10:20), the Lord says, "One thing you lack: Go your way, sell whatever you have and give to the poor, and you will have treasure in heaven; and come, take up the cross, and follow Me" (Mk. 10:21). Is the Lord telling the young man that he must give up everything he has in order to go to heaven?

In essence, Jesus Christ told the rich young ruler three things: 1) You must recognize who I am. That is the point of the question, "Why do you call me good? No one is good but One, that is God" (Mk. 10:18). In order to have eternal life one must recognize that Jesus Christ is God (Jn. 20:31). 2) You must know that you are a sinner in need of a Savior. That is why Jesus gave him the Law (Mk. 10:19). Jesus was using the Law lawfully (1 Tim. 1:8-11). The purpose of the Law was to reveal sin (Rom. 3:20). 3) You must cease trusting everything else and trust Me. That is why the Lord told the rich young ruler to sell what he had and give it to the poor.

After the young man walked away (Mk. 10:22), and the disciples expressed astonishment at what had taken place, Jesus told them, "Children, how hard it is for those who trust in riches to enter into the kingdom of God" (Mk. 10:24). In other words, Christ said that He told the rich young ruler to give away all of his goods, because he was *trusting* in his riches. The words "for those who trust in riches" are not in some manuscripts, but they are in the majority of manuscripts. The point Jesus was making had to do with faith. The young man needed to stop *trusting* in his riches so he could transfer his trust to Christ. So, Jesus told him he would be better off giving his riches away. Thus, the issue in the passage is not giving up material possessions. The issue is faith.

An ancient Jewish proverb states "whom the Lord loves he makes rich." The rich young ruler was of the opinion that God loved him and the proof of it was his riches. In that sense, he trusted his riches for eternal life. The analogous situation today would be like telling someone trusting their church membership for eternal life to cease trusting their church membership and start trusting Christ.

The invitation to "follow me" is a call to discipleship, not conversion. Notice carefully that had the rich young ruler done literally what Christ told him to do, he would have treasure in heaven *before* he followed Christ (Mk. 10:21). The young man's problem was that he trusted his money. The Lord told him to give that away. At that point, he would have trusted Christ and had treasure in heaven. Then, after faith, Christ invited him to "follow me," that is, become His disciple.

Summary: The New Testament does not teach sinners are saved by making Jesus the Lord of their life. The five arguments used to support Lordship Salvation are not the correct interpretation of the Biblical data.

Jesus did not practice Lordship Salvation. In John 4, He asked the Samaritan woman to give Him a drink of water (Jn. 4:7). When she objected, "Jews had no dealing with Samaritans" (Jn. 4:9), Jesus answered, "If you knew the gift of God, and who it is who says to you, 'Give Me a drink,' you would have asked Him, and He would have given you living water" (Jn. 4:10). She did not understand; she was still stuck on the literal water. So, she told Him, "Sir, You have nothing to draw with, and the well is deep. Where then do You get that living water?" (Jn. 4:11). Jesus clarified and she asked for the living water of which He spoke (Jn. 4:12-15).

This woman had been married five times and was living with a man to whom she was not married (Jn. 4:18). Jesus did not tell her she had to stop living with that man in order to receive eternal life. He did bring up the issue so that she would realize that she was a sinner in need of a Savior, but He did not tell her she even had to be willing to leave the man with whom she was living.

The remainder of the conversation concerned who Jesus is and the proper place of worship (Jn. 4:19-23). Finally, she said to Him "I know that Messiah is coming" (who is called Christ). "When He comes, He will tell us all things" (Jn. 4:25) and "Jesus said to her, 'I who speak to you am *He*" (Jn. 4:26).

The point is not that we should not tell people that God approves of or allows unmarried people living together. The point is that Jesus did not make that a *condition* for eternal life. All that is necessary for that is to drink of the water of life (Jn. 4:14) and that can be done by asking (Jn. 4:10). Based on what is said here, the requirement for receiving eternal life is realizing you are a sinner and recognizing that Jesus is the Messiah, ask God for the gift of eternal life. After a person has come to Christ for forgiveness, Jesus' word says, "Go and sin no more," as He told the woman caught in the act of adultery (Jn. 8:11), but in neither case did Jesus tell the individuals that *before* they came to Him for salvation.

Concerning the Samaritan woman, Ryrie says, "Plainly, she was living in sin. What an opportunity for the Lord to inject the matter of willingness to leave that immoral relationship in order to have living water (eternal life). What a great case study this woman could have been for all mastery advocates from that time to all this, but He had already told her what was necessary for her to have living water (John 4:10)—to know the gift (not reward) of God and who He was; then ask Him for that water. Even after some of the details of her sordid past and present came to light, Jesus did not change His message. He did not allow her to sidetrack Him with her question about where to worship, but he led that part of the dialogue back to the fact that He was the promised Messiah (verse 26). The Bible does not tell us whether or not the woman left her live-in man and mended her ways, but the record is crystal clear as to how she could have eternal life. Receive the gift of eternal life by asking Christ for it" (Ryrie, SGS, pp. 110-111).

Furthermore, it is possible to call Jesus "Lord" and claim to work miracles in His name and not be saved. Jesus said. "Not everyone who says to Me, 'Lord, Lord,' shall enter the kingdom of heaven, but he who does the will of My Father in heaven. Many will say to Me in that day, 'Lord, Lord, have we not prophesied in Your name, cast out demons in Your name, and done many wonders in Your name? And then I will declare to them, 'I never knew you; depart from Me, you who practice lawlessness!" (Mt. 7:21-23).

According to Jesus, the issue is not calling Him Lord or even working miracles in His name. It is doing the will of the Father to get to heaven, which is done by believing in Christ. Jesus made that clear when He said, "This is the will of the Father who sent Me, that of all He has given Me I should lose nothing, but should raise it up at the last day. And this is the will of Him who sent Me, that everyone who sees the Son and believes in Him may have everlasting life; and I will raise him up at the last day" (Jn. 6:39-40).

Preaching Lordship Salvation can easily mislead people into thinking *they* have to *do* something in order to be saved. In reference to the story of the Rich Young Ruler, Fromer writes, "The young man's question was 'Good Teacher, what must I do to inherit eternal life?' Essentially, Christ's answer was, 'Receive me as your Lord.' A difficulty may arise in the minds of some who are reading this. They have heard that they are saved by receiving Jesus as Savior. This incident however suggests that a man is saved when he enters upon a life of following Jesus, that is, when he receives Jesus as Lord." Fromer goes on to say, "So let's consider three areas where His Lordship will make a difference." He then discusses handing over one's possessions to their true owner, Jesus Christ, one's profession and one's relationship with the opposite sex" (Fromer, p. 5.).

One cannot read Fromer's article without coming to the conclusion that in order to be saved one must give over full control of his or her possessions to Christ, make a decision to let Christ determine what profession he will enter, and make a decision that he will marry only a Christian. Fromer has obviously taken the Lordship position to its logical extreme. Not all within that school of thought would go that far, but that is not uncommon either.

Ryrie related his experience in this regard. He tells of being accosted by a group of missionaries, who wanted to debate Lordship Salvation with him. After a long conversation, he says, he "asked about a hypothetical person who wanted to be saved, but he smoked. Furthermore, he knew full well that smoking was endangering his health, and he realized that if he became a Christian he ought to give it up. But he was unable to do so, nor was he even willing. So I asked these folks, 'Can he not be saved until either he gives up smoking or is willing to give up smoking?' Reluctantly they admitted that their view compelled them to say no, he cannot" (Ryrie, SGS, p. 113).

I once got into a discussion/debate with a proponent of Lordship Salvation. After some time I said, "I just want to see people saved. Please tell me what a person must do to be saved." He responded, "Last week I was witnessing to a fellow who was separated from his wife and I said to him, 'If I can show you in the Bible that it says you must go back to your wife, would you be willing to do that?' He said, 'No.' So I told him he could not be saved." Granted, not all who practice Lordship Salvation would go that far, but some do and *that is the danger of teaching Lordship Salvation.*

It should be clear by now that there are three entirely different opinions about salvation among evangelicals: True Grace, Decisionism and Lordship Salvation. The first issue is the condition or requirement for salvation. All three camps believe that salvation is by faith, but they mean different things by that and use radically different verses and ways to lead people to Christ.

Lordship Salvation defenders frequently charge those who believe in pure grace of believing in Decisionism. That is simply not true. Personally, I have been opposed to Decisionism since I was in college in 1960. I have had many personal conversations with the major leaders of the Free Grace movement of the later part of the twentieth century. There is no doubt in my mind that they do not believe nor practice Decisionism. Anyone who says they do, does not understand what the Free Grace people teach.

Part 2

The Certainty of Salvation

4

THE ASSURANCE
OF SALVATION

Believe it or not, the assurance of salvation is involved in the controversy over salvation. Can you imagine evangelicals disagreeing over the certainty of salvation?

From a True Grace perspective, this is the logical place to discuss the assurance of salvation, because it is part and parcel of saving faith. So, at this point, the True Grace position will be explained. In order to appreciate fully the Lordship Salvation view of assurance of salvation, a number of other concepts must be understood first. So, later, after those are explained, the Lordship Salvation view will be examined.

The Possibility of Assurance

The first thing that needs to be established is that the Bible teaches you can *know* you have eternal life. John says, "These things I have written to you who believe in the name of the Son of God, that you may know that you have eternal life, and that you may *continue to* believe in the name of the Son of God" (1 Jn. 5:13). Paul says, "I know whom I have believed and am persuaded that He is able to keep what I have committed to Him until that Day" (2 Tim. 1:12). It is not presumption to say that I know I have eternal life, that is, I know I am going to heaven.

It is not only possible to know that you saved; it is possible to know that you are saved the *day* you are saved. Jesus told a parable about two men, who went to the temple to pray (Lk. 18:10-13). The Pharisee thanked God that he was not "like other men; extortioners, unjust, adulterers, or even as this tax collector" (Lk. 18:11). The tax collector prayed, "God, be merciful to me a sinner!" (Lk. 18:13). Jesus says, "I tell you, this man went down to his house justified rather than the other." The implication is that the sinner went home knowing he was saved. A clearer case is the thief on the cross. When the thief said, "Lord, remember me when You come into Your kingdom" (Lk. 23:42), "Jesus said to him, 'Assuredly, I say to you, today you will be with Me in Paradise'" (Lk. 23:43). There is not doubt that the thief on the cross knew he was saved—the day he was saved. Jesus told him so.

The Basis of Assurance

The real issue is *how* can you know that you are saved? What is the basis of assurance? From a Biblical point of view, assurance is based on Christ's work and God's Word.

The Death of Christ When Christ died on the cross for our sins, He did everything necessary to get us to heaven. On the cross, He cried, "It is finished!" (Jn. 19:30). Our sin debt was paid in full. We can be assured of eternal life because Jesus died for our sins.

In his book, *Full Assurance*, Harry Ironside says our peace with God "rests not on me, not on my frames of my hand or experiences, but from the finished work of Christ and the testimony of the word of God" (Ironside, p. 8).

Referring to Isaiah 53, he writes, "'He was wounded for our transgressions.' Make it personal! Put yourself and your own sins in there. Read it as though it said, 'He was wounded for *my* transgressions.' Do not get lost in the crowd. If there had never been another sinner in the world, Jesus would have gone to the cross for you! Oh, believe it and enter into peace! 'He was bruised for our iniquities.' Make it personal! Think what your ungodliness and your self-will cost Him. He took the blows that should have fallen upon you. He stepped in between you and God, as the rod of justice was about to fall. It bruised Him in your stead. Again, I plead, make it personal! Cry out in faith, 'He was bruised for *my* iniquities.' Now go further. 'The chastisement of our peace was upon him.' All that was necessary to make peace with God, He endured. 'He made peace through the blood *of* his cross.' Change the 'our' to 'my.' 'He made *my* peace'" (Ironside, p. 20).

The Statements of Scripture To be assured of eternal life, simply take God at His Word. God's Word says, "Whoever believes in Him should not perish but have eternal life" (Jn. 3:15). "He who believes in the Son has everlasting life; and he who does not believe the Son shall not see life, but the wrath of God abides on him" (Jn. 3:36). "He who has the Son has life; he who does not have the Son of God does not have life" (1 Jn. 5:12). God said it. I believe it. That settles it.

One Greek professor says faith is "the inward conviction that what God says to us in the gospel is true" (Hodges AF, p. 31) and faith is "taking God at His Word. Saving faith is taking God at His Word in the gospel. It is nothing less than this. But it is also nothing more" (Hodges, AF, p. 32).

Francis Schaeffer agrees, "The Bible makes it plain that the man who is a Christian has a right to know that he is saved: it is one of a good gifts of God, to know truly that he is a Christian. This refers not only to the initial fact, after one has accepted Christ as Savior, it also applies to those great and crushing moments in our lives when the waves get so high that it seems, psychologically or spiritually, and we can never find our footing again. At such a moment, a Christian can have assurance. His salvation rests on the finished work of Christ whether he accepts the peace he should have or not; and he can have assurance to the extent to which he believes the promises of God at that moment" (Schaeffer, pp. 77-78).

Torrey says, "It is the blood of Christ that makes it safe; it is the word of God that makes it sure" (Torrey, pp. 480-481).

The Nature of Faith To say the same thing another way, assurance comes with faith. The traditional translation of Hebrews 11:1 is "Faith is the substance of things hoped for, the evidence of things not seen" (KJV, NKJV), but other translations render Hebrews 11:1: "Now faith is assurance of things hoped for, a conviction of things not seen" (ASV), "Now faith is the assurance of *things* hoped for, the conviction of things not seen" (NASB). "Now faith is being sure of what we hope for and certain of what we do not see" (NIV). Faith is being sure; it is assurance.

John Calvin (1509-64) teaches that faith includes assurance. He defines faith as "a firm and sure knowledge of the divine favor toward us, founded on the truth of a free promise in Christ and revealed to our minds, and sealed on our hearts, by the Holy Spirit" (Calvin, III, ii. 7). He calls faith a "full persuasion" of truth (Calvin, III. ii. 12) and speaks of being "firmly persuaded" (Calvin, III. ii. 6, II, ii. 16).

In his doctrinal dissertation at Oxford, later published under the title, *Calvin and English Calvinism to 1649*, R. T. Kendall came up with a similar list of expressions Calvin used to describe faith (Kendall, p. 19). He lists words such as "illumination" (Calvin, III. i. 4), "certainty" (Calvin, III. ii. 6), "firm conviction" (Calvin, III. ii. 16), "assurance" (Calvin, III. ii. 16), "firm assurance" (Calvin, III. ii. 16), and "full assurance" (Calvin, III. ii. 22). In other words, John Calvin captures the concept that faith is being persuaded and assured. Assurance comes with faith.

In *Systematic Theology*, Berkhof says that the reformers sometimes spoke as if "one who lacks the assurance of salvation did not possess true faith" (Berkhof, p. 507). He points out that the Heidelberg Catechism "conceives of the assurance of salvation is belonging to the essence of faith" (Berkhof, p. 507). Berkhof himself, a Reformed theologian, insists that faith includes an element of personal assurance (Berkhof, p. 505).

When you have trusted Christ, you *know* you have trusted Christ. How could you trust Christ without knowing it?

Summary: The basis of salvation is the finished work of Christ and the simple statement of Scripture. Assurance comes with faith.

Queen Victoria of England once heard a sermon that greatly impressed her. Later she asked her chaplain, "Is it possible to be absolutely sure in this life of eternal safety?" He replied, "I know of no way that one could be absolutely sure." This incident was later published in the Court News, which came to the attention of a minister by the name John Townsend. As a result, he sent the following letter to the Queen: "To her gracious Majesty, our beloved Queen Victoria, from one of her most humble subjects. With trembling hands but love-filled heart, and because I know that we can be absolutely sure even now of our eternal life in the home Jesus went to prepare, I would ask you, Most Gracious Majesty, to read the following passages of Scripture: John 3:16; Romans 10:9, 10. These passages prove there is full assurance of salvation by faith in our Lord Jesus Christ for those who believe and accept His finished work."

Several days later Townsend received this note: "Your letter of recent date received, and in reply would state that I have carefully and prayerfully read the portions of Scripture referred to. I believe in the finished work of Christ for me and trust by God's grace to meet you in that home of which He said, 'I go to prepare a place for you.'"

Victoria Guelph.

Part 3

The Consequences of Salvation

5
GOD-GIVEN FAITH

Thus far, the *requirement* for salvation and the *assurance* of salvation have been explained. Now the issues concerning the *results* of salvation will be explored.

Again, the True Grace view and the Lordship Salvation view are different. This is a complex part of the controversy involving a number of issues, such as: 1) faith (Does God gives some people faith?), 2) behavioral change (It is true that since God changes believers, so that they always manifest an immediate observable transformation of behavior?), 3) false faith (Does the New Testament speak of a false faith?), 4) faithfulness (Is it accurate to say that since God is working in believers, they will always endure to the end?), 5) fruit-inspectors (Does the New Testament teach that all believers produce discernable fruit so that by inspecting their lives one can tell if they are true believers?), and 6) faith-inspectors (Should believers examine their life to determine if they are saved?).

Instead of presenting the True Grace position and then the Lordship Salvation position, as has been done thus far, from this point on, the primary approach will be to analyze the various verses the Lordship Salvation advocates use to support their position. In the process, the True Grace exposition of those verses will be covered.

The core concept of Lordship Salvation is that real faith always produces immediately observable works and it endures to the end. That thesis is based on another one, namely, that God gives the repentance and faith necessary for salvation. In fact, the foundation of Lordship Salvation is the teaching that God gives repentance and faith. MacArthur states, "The heart of the debate deals with how much God does in redeeming the elect" (MacArthur, FW, p. 31).

The argument is that since real faith is God's gift, real faith will always manifest itself in observable works. Therefore, the first issue that needs to be addressed is whether God gives faith. A few passages in the New Testament seem to be saying He does. What are those passages and do they teach that God gives faith?

Ephesians 2:8

Paul says, "For by grace you have been saved through faith, and that not of yourselves; *it is* the gift of God" (Eph. 2:8).

Lordship Salvation View Some interpret the phrase "and that not of yourselves" in Ephesians 2:8 to mean that the *faith* is not of us (Chrysostom, Theodoret, Jerome, Augustine, Erasmus, Beza, Bengel). Bloomfield says, "All the Calvinistic commentators hold this view" (cited by Eadie, who adds that Calvin himself did not). Westcott writes, "*This* saving energy of faith is *not of yourselves: it is a gift*, and *the gift is God's*. Govett exclaims, "*Faith itself is the gift of God!*" Chafer concurs saying, "Even the faith by which it (salvation) is received is itself a *gift* from God" (Chafer, The *Ephesians Letter*, p. 79).

Charles Hodge claims that the middle clause of the verse is parenthetical and refers not to the main idea "you are saved," but to the subordinate one, namely, "through faith," and is designed to show how entirely salvation is of grace since even faith by which we apprehend the offered mercy, is the gift of God. He translates the verse, "You are saved through faith (and that not of yourselves it is the gift of God), not of works." He argues that to not handle the verse in this fashion makes it say the same thing over and over again without any progress. He also argues that the analogy of Scripture is in favor of this view because elsewhere faith is represented as a gift of God (1 Cor. 1:26-31, Eph. 1:19, Col. 2:12). His conclusion is "even faith is not of ourselves, it is the gift of God."

The Meaning of Ephesians 2:8 Ephesians 2:8 is not teaching that God gives believers faith (Calvin, Ellicott, Alford, Foulkes). Charles Hodge says that most *modern* commentators agree. The Greek word "faith" is in the feminine gender, as is the word "grace." The Greek word translated "that" is neuter. Therefore, "that" cannot refer to faith. It refers to the overall subject, which is salvation. It is salvation, which is not of us; salvation is of God." Alford contends that if "not of yourselves" is a reference to faith, "not of works" would be irrelevant and that the reference in verse 9 must be changed (see Eadie's explanation below). He states that salvation is the gift of God.

Robinson argues that the difference in gender is not fatal to the interpretation that "not of yourselves" is referring to faith, but he adds, "The context demands the wider reference." He goes on to say the phrase "not of works" shows that the subject is not faith, but salvation by grace.

Eadie points out that the pronoun "this" does not agree grammatically with faith. He says that the following verse indicates that faith is not the immediate reference. In his words, "You may say, 'And this faith is not of yourselves: it is God's gift;' but you cannot say, 'and this faith is not of yourselves, but is God's gift; not of works, lest any man should boast.' You would thus be obliged, without any cause, to change the reference in ver. 9, for you may declare that salvation is not of works, but cannot with propriety say that faith is not of works." He concludes that "not of works" must have salvation, and not faith, as its reference.

Calvin clearly concludes that the faith in Ephesians 2:8 is our part in salvation, not God's gift. He writes, "The next question is, in what way do men receive that salvation which is offered to them by the hand of God? The answer is, *by faith;* and hence he concludes that nothing connected with it is our own. If, on the part of God, it is grace alone, and if we bring nothing but faith, which strips us of all commendation, it follows that salvation does not come from us. Ought we not then to be silent about free-will, and good intentions, and fancied preparations, and merits, and satisfactions? There is none of these, which does not claim a share of praise in the salvation of men; so that the praise of grace would not, as Paul shows, remain undiminished. When, on the part of man, the act of receiving salvation is made to consist in faith alone, all other means, on which men are accustomed to rely, are discarded. Faith, then, brings a man empty to God, that he may be filled with the blessings of Christ. And so he adds, *not of yourselves;* that claiming nothing for themselves, they may acknowledge God alone as the author of their salvation." Calvin goes on to say, "Instead of what he had said, that their salvation is of grace, he now affirms, that "it is the gift of God." Note, Calvin taught "we bring nothing but faith" and salvation is the gift of God, not faith.

To sum up, while many commentators have claimed that Ephesians 2:8 is teaching the faith is a gift from God, a careful consideration of the text and the context indicates that such an interpretation is not correct.

Acts 5:31 and 11:18

Several passages in the New Testament speak of God granting repentance. "Him God has exalted to His right hand *to be* Prince and Savior, to give repentance to Israel and forgiveness of sins" (Acts 5:31). "When they heard these things they became silent; and they glorified God, saying, 'Then God has also granted to the Gentiles repentance to life'" (Acts 11:18). "In humility correcting those who are in opposition, if God perhaps will grant them repentance, so that they may know the truth" (2 Tim. 2:25).

The Lordship Salvation View Some commentators take these passage to mean that God gives repentance as a gift. Commenting on Acts 11:18, Bruce says that God gave them "through His Spirit a change of mind and heart and the assurance of eternal life." Concerning 2 Timothy 2:25, Hiebert says, "Only God can effect the change in them. He must 'give' it to them as a gift, using Timothy's efforts as a means to work the needed 'repentance' in them." Guthrie thinks that 2 Timothy implies that repentance is a gift from God.

The Meaning of Acts 5:31 Other commentators argue that these verses are simply saying that God gives people the *opportunity* to repent. The Greek word translated "grant" means, "to give," but it is used "in various senses" such as "bestow, grant, supply, deliver, commit, yield" (A-S, p. 114). Does this mean that God gives repentance as a gift? No. God giving Israel repentance (Acts 5:31) cannot mean that He gave the nation the gift of repentance. Only a few repented! Therefore, the expression "to give repentance to Israel" must mean that God gave the people of Israel the *opportunity* for repentance.

Commenting on Acts 11:18, Marshall says, through Jesus Christ. "the people of Israel might have the opportunity of repentance and of receiving forgiveness of their sins. Here is the offer of salvation to the very people who had crucified Jesus." Concerning Acts 11:18, he says that God "granted *to the Gentiles* as well as to the Jews the opportunity of repenting of their sins and thus of obtaining eternal life (5:20; 13:46, 48). This opportunity was provided in the preaching of the gospel."

Kent, a Greek professor, says that 2 Timothy 2:25 is saying, "By faithful teaching directed toward those who have set themselves in opposition to the truth (victims as well as the teachers), there is always the possibility that God would use the instruction to produce repentance."

Phillipians 1:29

Paul writes to the Philippians, "For to you it has been granted on behalf of Christ, not only to believe in Him, but also to suffer for His sake" (Phil. 1:29).

The Lordship Salvation View Muller states, "Such a faith ('the soul's going out to Christ in personal trust and hearty surrender') is a gift of grace, wrought in the heart by God's Spirit and granted by divine favor (Eph. 2:8)." Martin says, "The Philippians were called, not only to the privilege of believing in Him—the ability to believe and the act of faith being itself a gift of God—but equally to endure privation and pain *of* as did the apostle himself."

The Meaning of Philippians 1:29 Philippians 1:29 is not necessarily teaching that faith is a gift from God. It is simply saying that God in His grace is granting them the privilege of suffering as well as believing. Commentators use such language as a "double proof of His favor" (Alford), a "double grace of faith and suffering" (Eadie). MacDonald says, "The Philippians should remember that it is a privilege to suffer for Christ as well as to believe in Him" (MacDonald).

Eadie says, "The apostle is not teaching dogmatically that faith is of God's inworking; but he is telling historically that faith and suffering had been theirs, and that the coexistence of the two being a privilege of divine bestowment, warranted them to regard their undaunted belief as a token of salvation."

Kennedy writes, "To emphasize the real value of suffering for Christ's sake he compares it with that which they all acknowledged as the crowning blessing of their lives, faith in Him" (Kennedy, *The Expositor's Greek New Testament*).

Summary: A careful examination of the passages used to support the thesis that God gives repentance and faith does not sustain such a conclusion.

Faith comes by hearing (Rom. 10:17), not by regeneration! Does not the New Testament plainly place the responsibility to believe at the feet of sinners (Acts 16:31. cf. "we" in Acts 11:17)? God commands "all men everywhere to repent" (Acts 17:30). Moreover, the Bible is clear and consistent. When people believe, they receive life, not they receive life and after that faith.

6

GOD CHANGES PEOPLE

This core concept of Lordship Salvation is expressed a number of different ways, such as: discipleship is indispensable to salvation, justification and sanctification are inseparable, works are the inevitable result of faith, believers do not continue in sin, all believers produce fruit, etc. The argument is that since salvation is God's work (He gives people faith, He changes people), those who are saved will exhibit transformation. Speaking about the inseparability of justification and sanctification, MacArthur says that this question is "critical to the lordship debate" (MacArthur, FW, p. 90).

Does the New Testament say that God changes people? Does it teach that justification and sanctification are inseparable? Does it indicate that believers do not continue in sin?

Romans 6:6-7

In Romans, Paul develops the doctrine of justification by faith in detail (Rom. 1:18-5:21). Then, he describes, what happens to people who are justified by faith. Paul says, "We died to sin; how can we live in it any longer?" (Rom. 6:2) and "For we know that our old self was crucified with him so that the body of sin might be done away with, that we should no longer be slaves to sin because anyone who has died has been freed from sin" (Rom. 6:6-7). Simply put, those who are justified by faith are changed.

Lordship Salvation View The argument of Lordship Salvation is that since God changes them, there will be an immediate, observable change in behavior. "Any genuine transformation of the inner person must certainly affect outward behavior" (Saucy, p. 44). When MacArthur says, "Believers are free from sin and slaves of righteousness (6:18)" (MacArthur, FW, p. 31), he means all believers in every case. He says, "Real faith inevitably produces a changed life (2 Cor. 5:17)" (MacArthur, FW, p. 24).

Expressed theologically, this is the teaching that justification and sanctification are inseparable. The argument is that justification and sanctification can be distinguished, but they cannot be divorced. Many have embraced the inseparability of justification and sanctification. Calvin writes, "Christ, therefore, justifies no man without also sanctifying him. These blessings are conjoined by a perpetual and inseparable tie" (Calvin, 3:16:1). MacArthur says, "Justification never occurs alone in God's plan. It is always accompanied by sanctification" (MacArthur, FW, p. 104) and "Sanctification is inseparably linked to justification" (MacArthur, FW, p. 112).

More specifically, the argument is that Romans 6 teaches that believers have died to sin and, therefore, they *cannot* live in sin. MacArthur comments, "Christians have died to sin. It is therefore inconceivable to Paul that we might continue to live in sin from which we have been delivered by death" (MacArthur, FW, p. 113). He adds, "Dying to sin implies an abrupt, irreversible, wholesale break with the power of sin" (MacArthur, FW, p. 114). Morris contends that this inward, radical transformation delights to "spontaneously" produce the fruit of the Spirit.

The Meaning of Romans 6 There is no question that Paul is saying that believers died to sin and it is incongruous that believers live in sin, because they died to it (Rom. 6:2). When Paul asks, "What shall we say, then? Shall we go on sinning so that grace may increase?", his answer is "By no means!" (Rom. 6:1-2). To him, the thought of a believer living in sin was "abhorrent" (Lightfoot, Hodge) and "revolting" (Godet).

Paul goes on to say, "We died to sin; how can we live in it any longer?" (Rom. 6:2). He explains that those who are justified by faith have been spiritually baptized into Christ; they have been baptized into His death and resurrection (Rom. 6:3-5). When people trust Christ, they are "incorporated into" (Lightfoot, Sandy and Headlam), "united to" (Hodge), Jesus Christ. Being united to Jesus Christ means being united to His death and resurrection. His death and resurrection became *their* death and resurrection (Hodge).

What does Paul mean when he says, "we died to sin?" As he explains, "our old man is crucified with Him" (6:6). The word "man," does not refer to just part of a person, as if our old nature died, nor is Paul describing something that is only positionally true. What is described is actually true. The old man is the entire inner person, which lived prior to conversion (Alford, Murray). The old man is the man of old, the man who existed before conversion.

The man of old was crucified with Christ (Gal. 2:20). He has been put off (Col. 3:9, Eph. 4:22) and, therefore, he no longer exists. Simply put, believers in Jesus Christ are not the same people they were before conversion. They are new creatures (2 Cor. 5:17). Romans 6 definitely teaches that those who are justified by faith are changed.

God had two purposes in mind in crucifying the old man, as is indicated by the two clauses in Romans 6:6, which begin with "that" (Godet, Hodge, Murray). First, the old man was crucified "that the body of sin might be done away with" (Rom. 6:6a). "The body of sin" is the collective mass of sin (so Lightfoot, Hodge). Colossians 2:11, a parallel passage to Romans 6:6, indicates that the body of sin is the mass of sin. This mass of sin was abolished when the old man was crucified with Christ.

The second purpose was "that we should no longer be slaves to sin" (Rom. 6:6b). The old man who was a slave to sin was crucified.

The believer, who is now a new person, does not have to be a slave to sin (Hodge).

As Paul explains, "For he who has died and been freed from sin" (Rom. 6:7). Those who are spiritually dead in Christ are freed from sin. The word translated "freed" is the Greek word "justification," which is a forensic term. In a figurative sense, the word means, "freed." The idea is that believers no longer have any *legal obligation* to sin. Sin loses its case in court (Sandy and Headlam).

A slave owner has legal claims over a slave. The slave is legally obligated to obey, but if the slave has been legally freed, he is no longer obligated to obey. If the slave owner orders the slave to lie steal or kill the slave is entitled to answer, "My tongue and my hands no longer obey me" (Godet).

The fundamental thought in this passage is that believers have died to sin (Rom. 6:2, 6, 7). That is taken to mean, "A believer cannot therefore live in sin; if a man lives in sin he is not a believer" (Murray, p. 213). Murray concedes that "freed" from sin "will have to bear the forensic meaning." He even says, "Sin has no further claim upon the person." Nevertheless, he argues that the context deals with the deliverance from the power of sin.

Unquestionably, this passage is teaching that there is an inner change at conversion, but Paul's point is not that because there has been an inner change there will *always* be an immediate, observable change in behavior. He specifically says, "Our old man is crucified with Him ... that we *should* no longer be slaves to sin" (Rom. 6:6, italics added). In addition, when Paul says that we are "freed" from sin, he uses a forensic term, indicating that believers no longer have any *legal obligation* to sin.

It is blatantly obvious from Scripture as well as experience that believers are not dead to, nor freed from, sin. All believers sin (Jas. 3:1, 1 Jn. 1:8, 10). They should not. They are not obligated to sin. They can have victory over sin, *if* they do what the rest of this passage says, namely, reckon themselves dead to sin (Rom. 6:11) and present themselves to the Lord (Rom. 6:13), which means they obey Him

(Rom. 6:16). Paul does not assume this will happen. He exhorts them to "not let sin reign" in their mortal body (Rom. 6:12), indicating that if they do not do what Paul commands, sin will reign. To conclude anything less is not to take what Paul plainly says, seriously.

F. L. Godet (1812-1900) was a professor and "the greatest French commentator which evangelical Switzerland has produced" (J. Theodore Mueller of Concordia Theological Seminary). In his commentary on Romans, Godet says, "The *faith* of which the apostle speaks is nothing else other than the simple acceptance of the salvation offered in preaching. It is premature to put in this moral act all that will afterward flow from it when faith shall be in possession of its object.... (To do so) is to make the effect the cause. Faith, in Paul's sense, is something extremely simple such that it does not in the least impair the *freeness* of salvation" (Godet, p. 92).

1 John 3:9

John writes, "Whoever abides in Him does not sin. Whoever sins has neither seen Him nor known Him" (1 Jn. 3:6) and "Whoever has been born of God does not sin, for His seed remains in him; and he cannot sin, because he has been born of God" (3:9).

Lordship Salvation View A common explanation of these verses is that since "does not sin" is in the present tense, these verses mean true believers do not *practice* sin. For example, sin is not a "prevailing habit" (Westcott on 1 Jn. 3:6). Believers do "sin habitually and characteristically" (*Barnes Notes* on 3:9); they do not "do wrong deliberately and by design" (*Barnes Notes* on 3:6) and "If a man sins habitually, it proves that he has never been renewed" (*Barnes Notes* on 3:6). Sin "is not the constant course of his life" (Gill). Believers do not "continue to sin" (Stott). "The unbroken pattern of sin and enmity with God will not continue when a person is born again (I John 3:9-10)" (MacArthur, FW, p. 24).

Even the NIV translates, "No one who lives in Him keeps on sinning. No one who continues to sin has either seen Him or known Him" (1 Jn. 3:6) and "No one who is born of God will continue to sin, because God's seed remains in Him; he cannot go on sinning, because he has been born of God" (1 Jn. 3:9).

Are these verses teaching that believers do not practice sin? No. This explanation of the present tense has been criticized as not being a legitimate understanding of the present tense. Marshall says these interpreters stress the present tense here in a way they do not do elsewhere in the New Testament. He questions whether an important point of interpretation can be made on such a grammatical subtlety. Smalley calls this approach artificially stressing the continuous element in the present tense. Furthermore, if John had intended to convey the concept of not continuing to sin, he had Greek words he could have used and he did not (cf. Lk, 24:53, Heb. 13:15). Besides, 1 John 5:16 uses the present tense of the sins of believers.

The Meaning of 1 John 3:6, 9 Well, what do these verses mean? A number of other explanations have been suggested (see Marshall, Smalley). Taken at face value, the text itself explains itself. First John 3:6 says believers who *abide* in Christ do not sin. "Sin is not part of the experience of *abiding* in Christ (Bede, Brooke, Plummer). Moreover, sin is the result of blindness and ignorance toward God. In the act of sin, there is no vision of God. Every sin comes from an ignorance of God. First John 3:9 says that the regenerated self (cf. "born of God") cannot sin (Plummer, Hodges, in his commentary, *The Epistles of John*).

First John 3:9 consists of two statements, each of which is followed by an explanation (cf. "for" and "because"). The two statements are the one born of God 1) *does not* sin and 2) *cannot* sin. The explanations are God's seed remains in him and he is born of God. The question is, "What is the seed?" Marshall says most commentators take "seed" as a reference to the divine principle of life in the believer. For example, one commentary says his seed is "his higher nature, as one born or begotten of God, doth not sin. To be begotten of God and to sin, are states mutually excluding one another" (Jameson, Fausset and Brown). Hodges says that the "regenerated inner self" does not sin (cf. "inward man" in Rom. 7:22-23). As Hodges says, "If sin occurs, it is not the inward man who performs it."

Hebrews 12:14

The book of Hebrews says, "Pursue peace with all men, and holiness without which no one will see the Lord" (Heb. 12:14). The basic point is that believers are to pursue peace and holiness. The problem is the phrase that says without holiness no one will see the Lord.

Lordship Salvation View "See" has been interpreted as "to be in the presence of the Lord" (Westcott). MacArthur says, "The writer of Hebrews 12:14 states frankly that only those who continue living holy lives will enter the Lord's presence" (MacArthur, SWD, p. 151). If that is the case, the phrase "without which no one will see the Lord" means, that without holiness no one will be in the presence of the Lord, that is, go to heaven.

Taking that view, some conclude that practical holiness is a proof of salvation and that "if a person is not growing more holy, he is not saved" (MacDonald). It is argued that this verse teaches "sanctification is a *characteristic* of all those who are redeemed" (MacArthur, GAJ, p. 188).

The Meaning of Hebrews 12:14 "See" has been taken to mean communicating with the Lord (Guthrie mentions this possibility, cf. Mt. 5:8). Practical sanctification determines one's perception of God (Hodges).

Which interpretation is correct? Technically, it does not take practical holiness to be in the presence of God. Satan comes before God (Job 1) and all will one day bow their knee before Him (Phil.

2:10-11; see also Rom. 14:11, Rev. 1:7). So, this verse must mean that practical holiness allows one to see the Lord now (cf. Gen. 32:30, Ex. 24:9-11).

Summary: The passages used to teach that justification and sanctification are inseparable do not indicate that because there has been an inner change there will *always* be an immediate, observable change in behavior or that believers cannot live in sin.

Granted, believers are new creatures in Christ, but they do not always demonstrate immediate, perceivable change. There is such a thing as a secret disciple (cf. Joseph of Arimathea in Jn. 19:38). Ryrie remarks, "How long had he been a disciple before our Lord's crucifixion? We do not know for sure. But for some length of time Joseph had been both a member the Sanhedrin (Luke 23:50) and a secret disciple of Jesus. He did not consent to the Sanhedrin's decision to condemn Jesus, but that did not necessarily unmask him and reveal him as a follower of Jesus. He may simply have removed himself from the deliberation. Even when he asked permission to have the body of Jesus, his secret was not revealed to everybody" (Ryrie, SGS, p. 105).

God does not guarantee sanctification. In Romans 8, Paul says, "Moreover whom He predestined, these He also called; whom He called, these He also justified; and whom He justified, these He also glorified" (Rom. 8:30). Sanctification is omitted. God guarantees glorification, at least to some degree, but the text does not say He guarantees sanctification. Nevertheless, MacArthur's comment on this verse is, "Notice God's part in salvation begins with election and ends in glory. In between, *every aspect* of the redemptive process is God's work, not the sinner's. God will neither terminate the process nor omit any aspect of it" (italics added, MacArthur FW, p. 32,). MacArthur is simply reading into the verse more than is there. Sanctification is conspicuous by its absence!

7

REAL FAITH, FALSE FAITH

The backbone of the Lordship Salvation controversy is the inevitability of works. Lordship Salvation teaches that *real* faith *always* demonstrates observable works. All believers produce fruit. On the other hand, there is a false faith. False faith does not produce spiritual fruit. Does the New Testament teach that real faith always produces discernable works? Does it speak of a false faith?

James 2:14, 17

James says, "What *does it* profit, my brethren, if someone says he has faith but does not have works? Can faith save him?" (Jas. 2:14) and "Thus also faith by itself, if it does not have works, is dead" (Jas. 2:17). The message of these verses and, for that matter, the entire passage is that faith without works is dead. The question is, "What does that mean?"

Lordship Salvation View James 2 is a key passage in the lordship controversy. Based on the statement that faith without works is dead, the proponents of Lordship Salvation contend that there is a real faith and a false faith. The way to determine the difference between the two is works. According the Lordship Salvation view, real faith always produces works and false faith does not produce works.

In his epic work, *The Institutes of the Christian Religion*, John Calvin taught the concept of the false faith (Calvin, 3, II, 10-11). He speaks of a "shadow or image of faith," "a false semblance of faith" (Calvin, 3. II. 10) and a "fading faith" (3. II. 11). His explanation is that unbelievers are "sometimes affected in a way similar to the elect, that even in their judgment there is no difference between them. Hence, it is not strange, that by the Apostle a taste of heavenly gifts, and by Christ himself a temporary faith, is ascribed to them" (Calvin, 3. II. 11).

MacArthur says, "Real faith *inevitably* produces works" (MacArthur, FW, 149). He argues that James is teaching real faith "will no doubt produce righteous behavior" (MacArthur, FW, 142). On the other hand, MacArthur contends false faith does not produce works. "No works, no faith" (MacArthur, FW, 149). False faith is intellectual assent, "mere hearing, empty profession, demonic orthodoxy, and dead faith" (MacArthur, FW, 142).

The Meaning of James 2 James 2 is not talking about two kinds of faith. Granted, James says, "Someone *says* he has faith" (Jas, 2:14, italics added), but James does not mean this person's faith is not genuine faith. James addresses this passage to "my brethren" (Jas. 2:14, cf. Jas. 2:1, 15), that is, people who have exercised saving faith. The question at the end of the verse, "Can faith save him?" proves that James has a person with genuine faith in mind. The question is, "Can *faith* save?" That means the person has faith, real faith. Furthermore, "faith without works is dead," indicating it was once alive! The same Greek word translated "faith" here is used in James 5:15 of real faith. Plummer says that James "nowhere throws doubt on the truth of the unprofitable believer's professions." Dibelius says that the faith is that which Christians have. Even the faith of demons in this passage is real faith. They really believe there is one God (Jas. 2:19). That is not the faith that gets a person to heaven, but as far as it goes, it is real faith. What they did not do was *trust* Jesus Christ to get them to heaven. (By the way, the fact that the only thing the demons believed was monotheism renders their faith irrelevant to the issue of salvation. So says Ryrie in SGS, p. 122.)

The issue in this passage is not real faith versus false faith. It is *real* faith that is alone, meaning without works (Jas. 2:17), versus *real* faith that is not alone; it has works.

If the faith in James 2:14 is genuine faith that produces eternal life, what does James mean when he says, "Can faith save him?" (Jas. 2:14)?

The word "saved" occurs five times in the book of James (Jas. 1:21, 2:14, 4:12, 5:15, 5:20). Each time it refers to the saving of temporal life, not the saving of the eternal soul. For example, "soul" in James 1:21 means "life." James 5:15 says, "The prayer of faith will save the sick." Thus, James is not talking about going to heaven. He is simply asking, "Can faith without works save a person's *life* from something?" The question is, from what? The answer is, "Save your life from being wasted and possibly save it from death." James 2:14 must be kept in context. James 1:15 mentioned physical death. James 1:21 spoke of the saving of one's life from the defilement, destruction and death of sin. The Word is able to save your life (Hodges).

Also note, James 2:13 discusses the Judgment Seat of Christ. Then, in James 2:14, James asks, "What does it profit, my brethren, if someone says he has faith and does not have works?" In other words, what *profit* will believers have now and at the Judgment Seat of Christ if they do not produce works? James further asks, "Can faith save him?", that is, "Can faith without works save believers from wasting their lives now, possibly even dying, and being judged without mercy at the Judgment Seat of Christ?" Without works, a believer's life is wasted and not rewarded.

The issue is profit. Will a believer's life be profitable now so that he or she can be rewarded at the Judgment Seat of Christ or will it be unprofitable? A believer's life is unprofitable without love (1 Cor. 13:1-3) and without works (Jas. 2:14). In James 2, the works are acts of love and kindness (Jas. 2:8, 12, 15-16).

James 2 is not teaching that there is a real faith and a false faith. Nor is it saying that real faith always produces works. This passage is actually teaching the opposite of what the Lordship Salvation proponents are saying. James is teaching that it is possible to have genuine faith and not have works! He is urging believers to produce works.

James 2 teaches justification by faith. James says, "And the Scripture was fulfilled which says, 'Abraham believed God, and it was accounted to him for righteousness'" (Jas. 2:23). That is a quote from Genesis 15:6, the same verse, incidentally, which Paul uses to prove that justification is by faith (cf. Gal. 3:6, Rom. 4:3).

James 2 also teaches justification by works. James says, "Was not Abraham our father justified by works when he offered Isaac his son on the altar?" (Jas. 2:21). That is a reference to Genesis 22:9, 12. In Genesis 15, Abraham was justified by faith. Years later, in Genesis 22, Abraham was justified by works when he offered Isaac on the altar. Justification by faith is before God. Paul says, "For if Abraham was justified by works, he has something of which to boast, *but not before God*" (Rom. 4:2, italics added). Justification by works is *before people* (cf. "you see" in Jas. 2:22).

James concludes, "Do you see that faith was working together with his works, and by works faith was made perfect?" (Jas. 2:22). In the case of Abraham, faith was *working together* with works to *perfect* faith. The word "perfect" does not mean, "without fault or flawless." It means "full grown, mature." As Abraham worked, that is, as he offered Isaac on the altar, his faith grew and matured.

The point of James 2 is that if people have genuine faith in Christ and do not perform works, their faith is dead, that is inactive. If, however, their faith is active, they will work and those works will mature their faith.

In fact, there is a textual problem in James 2:20. The *Textus Receptus* Greek text and the *Majority Text* say, "faith without works is dead," but the Critical Text says "faith without works is useless" (cf. NASV, NIV). The Greek word translated "useless" means, "inactive, idle, lazy". It is used in 2 Peter 1:8 (cf. "barren"). Commenting on the NASV translation of 2 Peter 1:8, which uses the translation "useless," MacArthur says, "The word translated 'useless' is used in the discourse on dead faith in James 2. If you add virtue in your life, you won't be dead in terms of your effectiveness" (MacArthur, SWD, p. 125). Using MacArthur's text and logic, would not one conclusion be that James 2:20 is saying that faith without works is useless, that is, inactive, idle, lazy?

Richard A. Seymour points out that a car battery illustrates the point of this passage. He says, "If I told you that the battery in my minivan is dead, I wouldn't mean that I didn't have a battery (nonexistent); I would mean that it was not producing juice; there would be no power coming from it. The battery would be there under the hood where it is supposed to be. It just would be in a temporary condition of being useless insofar as it being effective in turning over the motor when I turn the key in the ignition. So it is in James: the 'dead' faith is a non-producing faith, a barren, an unfruitful faith—but faith, nonetheless."

The New Testament teaches that believers *should* work, not that they will automatically work. Paul says, "For we are His workmanship, created in Christ Jesus for good works, which God prepared beforehand that we should walk in them" (Eph. 2:10). Notice that Paul says, "should," not will.

Paul also states, "This is a faithful saying, and these things I want you to affirm constantly, that those who have believed in God should be careful to maintain good works. These things are good and profitable to men" (Titus 3:8). The Greek word translated "affirm constantly" implies persistence and thoroughness (Alford). Far from works being automatic, Paul taught that believers needed to be constantly and continuously told to work.

Furthermore, believers will have to put forth thought and effort. They are to be "careful" to do so. The word "careful" means, "to take thought to" and it denotes earnest and careful thought; yea, even a straining in that direction (Fairbairn). They should be concerned and careful to "maintain" good works. The Greek word rendered "maintain" means, "to stand before, preside over, rule, govern," but here probably simply means, "direct, maintain, practice." They were to have a thoughtful approach to maintaining good works (Guthrie). The point is that those who are trusting in God need to be constantly told they should give thought and effort to continually practicing good works. In short, they should plan and perform good works.

When it comes to works, there are three "theological" opinions. Calvinism teaches that true believers *will* work and if they do not they were never saved. Arminianism teaches that believers *must* work and if they do not, they lose their salvation. True Grace teaches that believers *should* work and if they do not, they lose rewards. Note the word "should" in Ephesians 2:10 and Titus 3:8.

John 15:2

Jesus says, "I am the true vine, and My Father is the vinedresser. Every branch in Me that does not bear fruit He takes away; and every branch that bears fruit He prunes, that it may bear more fruit. You are already clean because of the word which I have spoken to you" (15:1-3). Obviously, the Lord is talking about two kinds of branches, those that do not produce fruit and those that do.

Lordship Salvation View Based on the assumption that believers always produce fruit, the Lordship Salvation interpretation of this passage is that the unfruitful branches are unbelievers. MacArthur says, "Since all Christians bear some fruit, it is clear that the fruitless branches in John 15 cannot refer to them" (MacArthur, SWD, p. 32). Morris says that the unfruitful branches had close contact with Jesus, but they were not true disciples. Judas is an example (Morris in a fn., p. 670).

The Meaning of John 15 It is obvious that in this passage the branches are believers. Jesus says "every branch *in Me*" (Jn. 15:2, italics added), not "in the church" or "in Christendom." He clearly calls the disciples branches (Jn. 15:5). The unfruitful believers are cast forth "as branches" (Jn. 15:6). Westcott says, "Even the unfruitful branches are true branches. They also are 'in Christ,' though they draw their life from Him only to bear leaves." Plummer agrees, "that is, everyone who is by origin a Christian." Therefore, both fruitful and unfruitful branches are believers.

If interpreters come to this passage with a theological presupposition that there is no such thing as an unfruitful believer, their only logical conclusion is that the branches are not believers. That theological presupposition, however, is false. After telling believers to add various virtues to their faith, Peter says, "For if these things are yours and abound, *you will be* neither barren nor unfruitful in the knowledge of our Lord Jesus Christ. For he who lacks these things is shortsighted, even to blindness, and has forgotten that he was cleansed from his old sins" (2 Pet 1:8-9). According to the Apostle Peter, it is possible for those who has been purged from their old sins to "lack these things," meaning they are unfruitful. Except for the theological presupposition that it is impossible for a believer to not bear fruit, one would never conclude that the unfruitful branch in John 15:2 is not a Christian.

The unfruitful branch is "taken away." The Greek word translated "takes away" can mean either lift up (Jn. 8:59) or take away, remove (Jn. 2:16). It is used in John 5:8-12 of picking up one's bed and in John 8:59 of picking up stones. The allegory in this passage indicates that here it has the meaning of lifting up. When a branch was unfruitful, the vinedresser did not immediately remove it. He would always try to salvage the branch first by lifting it up and propping it on a stick so it could get more sunlight. When God the Father, the loving vinedresser, finds a branch that is unproductive, His first response is to take steps to make it fruitful. Ryrie says, "God encourages the fruitless person to bear fruit by exposing him or her to the sunshine of life" and "He lifts them up in blessing and guidance, positioning them so that they can bear fruit" (Ryrie, SGS, p. 52).

John 10:27-28

Jesus says, "My sheep hear My voice, and I know them, and they follow Me. And I give them eternal life, and they shall never perish; neither shall anyone snatch them out of My hand" (10:27-28). Jesus says that His sheep hear His voice and follow Him.

Lordship Salvation View The Lordship Salvation defenders use this verse to say that genuine believers always follow Christ. "All true believers follow Jesus (John 10:27-28)" (MacArthur, FW, p. 24).

The Meaning of John 10 The point of this passage is that Jesus told unbelievers in Jerusalem (Jn. 10:25) that if they were in sympathy with Him and His Father, they would believe in Him and would receive those supreme and eternal blessings, which He could impart. In the process of saying this, the Lord describes three characteristics about His sheep.

First, His sheep hear His voice (Jn. 10:27a). Several shepherds placed their sheep in the same sheepfold for the night. The next morning the shepherd would call his sheep and they, knowing his voice, would respond because they were his (cf. Jn. 10:4).

Second, His sheep follow Him (Jn. 10:27b-28a). Christ's sheep hear and heed. What does it mean to follow? This is normally taken to mean discipleship. In other passages, that's true, but here it is not. Notice carefully. He does not say, "I give unto them eternal life and they follow," but rather, "They follow Me and I give unto them eternal life." Therefore, "following" in this passage must be a metaphor for faith. In other passages in the Gospel of John, metaphors for faith include coming (Jn. 6:35-37), eating bread (Jn. 6:35) and drinking (Jn. 4:14). In this verse, the Lord says He gives unto them eternal life (present tense), not I will give them eternal life (future tense). In this passage, eternal life is not a promise to be fulfilled later; it is a gift to be received now.

Hodges writes, "When the shepherd calls the sheep through His Word (and they know who they are!), they respond to that call by following Him. That is to say, they commit their safety and well-being to the shepherd who has summoned them to do so. A sheep's instinctive fear of strange voices lies, of course, in the background of the metaphor (see Jn. 10:4-5), so that the decision to follow is after all an act of trust" (Hodges, *The Gospel Under Siege*, pp. 44-45).

Third, His sheep never perish (Jn. 10:28). The phrase "they shall never perish" is literally, "shall certainly not perish forever." In the Greek text, there is a double negative plus the phrase "forever." This is one of the most emphatic statements in the New Testament. Furthermore, no one shall snatch them out of His hand. The word "snatch" literally means, "to snatch away or carry off by force." It is the same word used of the wolves in verse 12.

Summary: The major passages used to say that the New Testament teaches that real faith always demonstrates discernable works and there is a false faith, do not contain such a concept.

This is not a question of whether or not the New Testament speaks of *false brethren*. There are false brethren in the New Testament (2 Cor. 11:26, Gal. 2:4). The question is not about the possibility of people today making a "profession" (Decisionism) without being regenerate. That can and does happen. The issues are, "Does the New Testament teach that real faith always demonstrates discernable works?" "Does it speak of a false faith?" The answer is, "No."

There are other passages pertaining to the issue of false faith in the New Testament. Those will be examined later in the chapter entitled, "By Their Fruits."

8
THOSE WHO ENDURE

Lordship Salvation preachers insist that genuine believers not only immediately manifest a transformed life and produce good works and fruit, they also endure to the end of their lives (Mt. 24, Jn. 8, 1 Jn. 2:19). What God begins He will finish (Phil. 1:6). When real believers fall, they get up. If they do not, they were never saved.

For example, MacArthur writes, "Those whose faith is genuine will prove their salvation is secure by persevering to the end in the way of righteousness and. . . true believers will persevere. If a person turns against Christ, it is proof that person was never saved. . . no matter how convincing a person's testimony might seem, once he becomes apostate he has demonstrated irrefutably that he was never saved" (MacArthur, GAJ, p. 98). It is not that a Christian never sins "but rather that when he does sin he inevitably returns to the Lord to receive forgiveness and cleansing" (MacArthur, GAJ, p. 104). In another book, MacArthur writes, "If a person leaves the fellowship of God's people and never comes back, he or she was never a true believer to begin with" (MacArthur, SWD, p. 33).

As someone else has said, "The faith that fails before it finishes was flawed from the first."

Matthew 10:22, 24:13

When Jesus sent out the Twelve to Israel, He told them, "And you will be hated by all for My name's sake, but he who endures to the end will be saved" (Mt. 10:22b). Also in the Olivet Discourse, He said, "But he who endures to the end shall be saved" (Mt. 24:13).

The Lordship Salvation View The statement "he who endures to the end shall be saved" is often taken to mean those who persevere in their spiritual life will be saved spiritually.

The Meaning of Matthew 10:22 and 24:13 In both Matthew 10:22 and 24:13, Jesus is speaking about the Tribulation prior to His Second Coming. In Matthew 10, it is apparent that Jesus is speaking about the Tribulation because at the beginning of the discourse He tells them to go to Israel (Mt. 10:6) and not to go into the way of the Gentiles (Mt. 10:5-6), but later in the passage He tells them they will be brought before Gentiles (Mt. 10:18), the Holy Spirit has already come (Mt. 10: 20) and the events in this part of the passage take place just prior to the Second Coming (Mt. 10:23)! Wiersbe points out that Jesus even speaks of ministry to the Gentiles (Mt. 10:18) and a worldwide persecution (Mt. 10:22). He adds, "It is difficult to escape the conclusion that these instructions apply to witnesses at some future time." He concludes, "The period described in this section closely parallels the time of tribulation" (cf. "he who endures to the end will be saved" in Mt. 10:22).

There is no doubt that Mathew 24:13 is referring to the Tribulation prior to the Second Coming. In that passage, Jesus says, "Immediately after the tribulation of those days the sun will be darkened, and the moon will not give its light; the stars will fall from heaven, and the powers of the heavens will be shaken. Then the sign of the Son of Man will appear in heaven, and then all the tribes of the earth will mourn, and they will see the Son of Man coming on the clouds of heaven with power and great glory" (Mt. 24:29-30).

The problem with the explanation is that "they who endure to the end" means those that persevere in their spiritual life will be saved spiritually is that the subject of both passages is not spiritual salvation. The subject under discussion is service, not salvation.

Therefore, "endurance" in these passages is enduring the persecution of the Tribulation and being "saved" is deliverance. Alexander says those who persist in the faith in extreme trials will be "rescued, finally delivered from them." They must endure arrest, scourging, trials before religious and civic leaders, as well as rejection by their own families. Wiersbe says, "The tribulation will be a time of opposition and opportunity." He adds, "No matter how difficult our circumstances may be, we can turn opposition into opportunities for witness" and "Instead of fleeing and looking for an easier place, we can 'endure to the end,' knowing that God will help us and see us through." According to McNeile, endurance in this passage is enduring the "intensity of the persecution" and salvation is "deliverance and victory in the coming kingdom." He says the best commentary on this verse is Revelation 2:10.

John 8:31

John 8 says, "As He spoke these words, many believed in Him. Then Jesus said to those Jews who believed Him, 'If you abide in My word, you are My disciples indeed. And you shall know the truth, and the truth shall make you free'" (8:30-32). In short, Jesus said, "If you abide, you are My disciple indeed."

The Lordship Salvation View Some argue that these believers were not genuine believers. To support their claim, they point to what they say is a weak construction for "believe" in the Greek text (Tasker). MacArthur sites John 8:31 as one of the verses that supports his contention that "those who obey His word are the true believers" (MacArthur, FW, p. 121). Notice that MacArthur says "believers." Jesus did not say those who abide are true believers; He said they were true disciples. (In MacArthur's view, there is no difference between a believer and a disciple.)

The Meaning of John 8:31 In the first place, there is no doubt that this passage is talking about genuine believers. In the Greek text, "believed in Him" (Jn. 8:30) is regarded by many as the strongest possible Greek construction for "believe." Since John 8:31 is in response to genuine believers in John 8:31, the believers in verse 31 are true believers. Furthermore, Jesus does not say those who continue in His word are *believers*; He says they are His disciples. The Greek word translated "disciple" means, "learner." His point is that if *believers* obey His word, they shall be *disciples*. Rather than a proof text for Lordship Salvation, this verse supports the teaching that there is a difference between salvation and discipleship.

1 John 2:19

The Apostle John writes, "They went out from us but they were not of us; for if they had been of us they would have continued with us; but they went out that they might be made manifest that none of them were of us" (1 Jn. 2:19). In the context of 1 John 2, John is saying that the antichrists (cf. 1 Jn. 2:18) went out from "us" because they were not of us.

The Lordship Salvation View A common interpretation of 1 John 2:19 is that the antichrists went out "from us," that is, the Christian community, because they were not "of us," that is, they were not Christians (Plummer, Stott, Marshall). MacArthur says, "Those who later turn completely away from the Lord show that they were never truly born again (1 John 2:19)" (MacArthur, FW, p. 25).

The Meaning of 1 John 2:19 The question is, "Who is the 'us' in 1 John 2:19?" It is generally assumed that it is a reference to the Christian community, but that view misunderstands the meaning of "us" in this epistle. In the opening verses, John made a definitive distinction between we/us and you. The we/us were the eyewitnesses of Christ, that is, the apostles, while the "you" were, of course, the readers (cf. 1 Jn. 1:1-5). That same distinction is maintained in this passage, for in the next verse John refers to the readers as "you." Therefore, the "us" of 1 John 2:19 is a reference to the apostolic circle (cf. also "you," "they," "us" in 1 Jn. 4:1-6).

"Of us" does not mean source of the being, but source of the attitude and actions, their persuasion and position. That is obvious from John's use of this same construction in 1 John 3:8 where he says everyone who sins is "of the devil," that is, all sin is of the devil. Yet, that does not mean that everyone who sins has the devil as his source of being. It only means that one who sins has the devil as the ultimate source of his sin. That must be what John means, because a believer can hate his brother (2:9), but such action is not "of God" (1 Jn. 3:10, cf. also 1 Jn. 3:19). Thus, John is saying that these antichrists departed from the apostolic churches of Jerusalem and Judea (Hodges, *Bible Knowledge Commentary*, p. 891), but they were not of the apostolic persuasion.

John goes on to explain (cf. "for") that if they had been in harmony with the apostolic doctrine, they would have remained (the Greek word translated "continued" is the word usually rendered "abide") in fellowship with the apostles (1 Jn. 1:1-3). Had they been "of God" they would have submitted to the apostolic doctrine (1 Jn. 4:6). Their departure revealed they were not of the apostolic doctrine. Their departure unmasked them (Law).

Phillipians 1:6

Paul says, "Being confident of this very thing, that He who has begun a good work in you will complete it until the day of Jesus Christ" (Phil. 1:6). Paul was persuaded that God had started something, a good work, and He would finish it.

The Lordship Salvation View Many take the "good work" as the comprehensive work of God in the believer and conclude that this verse is teaching the perseverance of the saints (Bruce). After citing Philippians 1:6, MacArthur says, "Salvation is wholly God's work, and He finishes what He starts" (MacArthur, FW, p. 33).

The Meaning of Philippians 1:6 The question is, "What is the good work?" The immediate context seems to suggest that the "good work" is their cooperation with Paul in the gospel. Lightfoot states, "By this 'good work' is meant their cooperation with and affection for the apostle." Martin, who does not agree with that explanation, admits it is possible and adds, "2 Corinthians 8:6 uses almost identical verbs 'begin, finish' for Titus' administration of the relief fund for the Jerusalem church."

Eadie points out that this statement "refers to a particular action, and is not in itself a general statement of a principle." The Philippians decided to do the good work of giving to Paul's ministry, but it was God who began it and He was the One working in them (Phil. 2:12-13). Giving is a grace (2 Cor. 8:7). Paul is confident that what God started He will finish. Since He began the good work of this gift, He will complete it until Christ comes. Hodges suggests that this good work of a contribution to Paul's ministry produced this very letter, which will continue until Christ returns (Hodges, *The Gospel under Siege*, pp. 88-89).

Summary: The passages used to teach that all believers always endure to the end do not teach that idea.

The Lordship Salvation explanation of endurance is that since God is the One who saves, all believers endure. MacArthur argues "Grace transforms a person's innermost being" and "No true believer will continue indefinitely in disobedience, because sin is diametrically opposed to our new and holy nature. Real Christians cannot endure perpetually sinful living" (MacArthur, FW, p. 121). Such an interpretation is built on logic, not on the statements of Scripture.

What does the Scripture *say* about endurance? Is endurance automatic? Do all believers endure to the end of their lives?

In the New Testament, believers are *commanded* to endure. Paul told Timothy, "But you, O man of God, flee these things and pursue righteousness, godliness, faith, love, patience, gentleness" (1 Tim. 6:11). The Greek word translated "patience" here is the same Greek word rendered endurance. It is the same one that is used in Matthew 10:22 and Matthew 24:13. The writer to the Hebrews says, "Therefore we also, since we are surrounded by so great a cloud of witnesses, let us lay aside every weight, and the sin which so easily ensnares *us,* and let us run with endurance the race that is set before us" (Heb. 12:1. See also Heb. 10:36). Peter exhorts believers to add endurance to their faith (2 Pet. 1:6, where the word translated "perseverance" is the Greek word for "endurance").

Furthermore, it is tribulation that produces endurance (Rom. 5:3, Jas. 1:4). Granted, believers must depend upon the grace of God to endure, but endurance is not simply based on the fact that believers have a new nature. They must cooperate with the grace of God, an emphasis that is lacking in the Lordship Salvation approach to Scripture.

In the New Testament, believers are exhorted not to fall away. The writer to the Hebrews says, "Beware, brethren, lest there be in any of you an evil heart of unbelief in departing from the living God" (Heb. 3:12). According to Lordship Salvation, it is not possible for true believers to fall away. That interpretation of the Scripture renders the warnings against falling away, such as is in Hebrews 13:12, meaningless.

In the New Testament, there is a sin unto death, which indicates that not all believers endure in sanctification to the end (See 1 Jn. 5:16, 1 Cor. 11:30, Acts 5:1-11).

In the New Testament, some believers do not even endure in faith. Paul says, "If we endure, we shall also reign with *Him.* If we deny *Him,* He also will deny us. If we are faithless, He remains faithful; He cannot deny Himself" (2 Tim. 2:12-13). The Greek word translated "faithless" means, "to disbelieve, be faithless." In *The King James Version*, it is translated, "if we believe not." Notice, Paul includes himself (cf. "we"). The point is regardless of what believers do, even if they cease to believe, God cannot deny His nature or His promises.

Concerning this passage, Guthrie says, "Christ's constancy to His own promise provides a believer with his greatest security. It is unthinkable that any contingency could affect the faithfulness of God, for He cannot deny Himself." Litfin writes, "He will not deny even unprofitable members of His own body. True children of God cannot become something other than children, even when disobedient and weak. Christ's faithfulness to Christians is not contingent on their faithfulness to Him." Kent observes, "Though Christians are often faithless, even as Peter was, Christ remains faithful to us, to His promises, and to His own unchanging nature."

Ryrie says this passage is "no warning of certain condemnation to false professors." He goes on to point out that Ellicott, a 19th century Greek scholar, says there is no sufficient reason for departing from the regular meaning of "faithless," that is, "unbelief." Ryrie concludes, "According to Ellicott, apparently a believer can come to the place of not believing, and yet God will not disown him, since He cannot disown Himself" (Ryrie, SGS, p. 141).

Hodges states, "Let there be no mistake. The failure of one's faith is a grim possibility on the field of spiritual battle. To deny this is to be spiritually unprepared for the enemy's assault" (Hodges, AF, p. 111).

9
BY THEIR FRUITS

According to the Lordship Salvation interpretation of the New Testament, since justification and sanctification are inseparable, since real faith always produces observable works and since believers always endure to the end, therefore, by their fruits, you shall know them (Mt. 7:16).

To say the same thing another way, the test of real faith is fruit. There is a false faith. Those who *profess* faith, but who do not produce good works, did not have saving faith. So, the way to determine if a profession is real faith or false faith, look at the person's life. If there is fruit, there is real faith. If there is no fruit, fruit that endured, the faith was not real faith; it was false faith. A person can be a professor and not a possessor. If there is no change in a person's life, we have the right to question that they were saved.

So, in several passages in the New Testament that say people believed, commentators look at what happened after that and based on the person's life, *not the plain statement that they believed*, commentators conclude those individuals were never saved; they had false faith (Lk. 8:13, Jn. 2:23-24, Acts 8:13).

As was pointed out earlier, this is not a question of whether or not the New Testament speaks of false brethren. There are false brethren in the New Testament (2 Cor. 11:26, Gal. 2:4). It is about passages that say people *believed.* The issue is, "When the New Testament says that someone believed, is it possible it does not mean what it says?

Matthew 7:16

Jesus said, "You will know them by their fruits" (Mt. 7:16). Does that statement not mean that real faith always produces observable fruit?

The Lordship Salvation View The Lordship interpretation of this passage is that "them" is all believers and "fruits" refers to the behavior of believers. Thus, this statement is often used as a test to determine people's salvation. Commenting on this verse, Wiersbe says, "True faith in Christ changes the life and produces fruit for God's glory."

The Meaning of Matthew 7:16 The subject of Matthew 7:15-20 is not all believers; it is false prophets. The passage begins with Jesus saying, "Beware of false prophets" (Mt. 7:15a). Having said that few find the narrow way (Mt. 7:14), Jesus is now saying that if you wish to find the narrow way, you must beware of "untrustworthy guides" (Plummer).

Jesus goes on to say that these false prophets "come to you in sheep's clothing, but inwardly they are ravenous wolves" (Mt. 7:15). They approach people "claiming to be like themselves," harmless sheep. At first, their teaching appears to bear resemblance to the truth (Tasker). What they say seems plausible, enabling them to pass as prophets. The truth is they are not what they appear to be. Instead of being harmless sheep, they are destructive wolves, who are the natural enemy of sheep. They are ravenous. The Greek word translated "ravenous" means, "rapacious, swindler, extortioner." "They are greedy of gain and power" (Plummer). False prophets are in the ministry for what they get, not for what they can give (Barclay). They exploit people, not edify them (Wiersbe).

Jesus gives the test of a false prophet. "You will know them by their fruits. Do men gather grapes from thorn bushes or figs from thistles?" (7:16). The test of a *false prophet* is his fruit. Some apply the fruit-test to everyone, not just false prophets. For example, France says, "Here it relates specifically to false prophets, but the principle would apply equally to any Christian profession." The problem with that conclusion is that there is not so much as a hint in this passage that Jesus intended for it to be applied to everyone. As given by Jesus, in this passage the fruit-test is about false prophets (cf. Mt. 7:22).

In addition, the fruit is often taken to be character (Alexander, Tasker, France). In his commentary on the Sermon on the Mount, Haddon Robinson points out, "We assume Jesus was saying that we can identify good people by their good deeds, by the lives they live. But having studied so much of the Sermon on the Mount, we know that cannot be what Jesus was teaching. In fact, some of those he singled out as being false prophets, the Pharisees and the scribes, kept all the religious rules and regulations. If 'fruit' means the same as 'good works,' the Pharisees would be the first to qualify for a medal of righteousness."

What, then, is the fruit-test? The fruit of an apple tree is an apple. Likewise, the fruit of a prophet is prophecy (Robinson). Later in His ministry, Christ used the fruit-test illustration and there fruit is clearly "words" (Mt. 12:33, cf. Mt. 12:32, 34. 36, 37). The test of a false prophet is the fruit of a false prophet, which is what the false prophet teaches.

Luke 8:13

Jesus says, "Now the parable is this: The seed is the word of God. Those by the wayside are the ones who hear; then the devil comes and takes away the word out of their hearts, lest they should believe and be saved. But the ones on the rock *are those* who, when they hear, receive the word with joy; and these have no root, who believe for a while and in time of temptation fall away" (Lk. 8:11-13).

In explaining the parable of the sower, Jesus made it clear that the seed that fell upon the path represents those who did not get saved (Lk. 8:12). They did not *believe* and did not get saved. If they had believed, they would have been saved. On the other hand, the seed that fell upon rocky ground represents those who believe for a while, but later fall away (Lk. 8:13).

Not Genuine Believers The question is, "Are the people who believed for a while saved?" Most commentators claim that they were not saved, because they only believed *for awhile*.

In his commentary, Calvin says that the "honor which they render to the Gospel resembles faith," but that "they are not truly regenerated." He goes on to say that they "take delight in the word of God, and cherish some reverence for it, do in some manner *believe;* for they are widely different from unbelievers, who give no credit to God when he speaks, or who reject his word. In a word, let us learn that none are partakers of true faith, except those who are sealed with the Spirit of adoption, and who sincerely call on God as their Father; and as that Spirit is never extinguished, so it is impossible that the faith, which he has once engraven on the hearts of the godly, shall pass away or be destroyed."

Geldenhuys says they only received the Word with emotional excitement and superficial enthusiasm; they did not allow the seed of the Word to penetrate deeply into their hearts. According to him, they were not genuinely converted; they were only temporarily taken up with the preaching of the Word.

Genuine Believers In Luke 8:12 Jesus said if people believed they would be saved. Then, He speaks of people who believed for a while (Lk. 8:13). If the word "believe" in Luke 8:12 is saving faith, the word "believe" in Luke 8:13 is also saving faith. There is no indication in the text or context that the meaning of the word "believe" changed from one verse to another.

Furthermore, they received the word. The Greek word translated "receive" means, "to receive, accept." It is used of "taking what is offered" (A-S). It is same word that is used in 1 Corinthians 2:14, where it is said that the *natural man does not receive* the things of the Spirit of God, that is, the Word of God. Plummer states that this Greek word for receive implies internal acceptance. Dillow argues that the expression "receive the word" is "a virtual synonym for a salvation experience" (Dillow, p. 398). Dillow quotes no less than Link, who says that the expression "to receive the word," became " a technical term for the believing acceptance of the gospel" (H. G. Link, "Take" in NIDNTT, 3:746).

Besides, the seed that fell upon the rocky ground was able to germinate; life sprang up, but the soil lacked moisture (Lk. 8:6). Note, the seed *geminated*; life sprang up.

Temporary Believers The only possible indication that they were not saved is that they believed *for awhile* and later fell away. As has been pointed out, these are genuine believers. Therefore, the question becomes, "Can a genuine believer fall away?"

The Greek word translated "fall away" in Luke 8:13 means, "to stand off, depart from, withdraw from, fall away, apostatize, withdraw oneself from." It is used of genuine believers in the Hebrews 3:12, which says, "Beware, brethren, lest there be in any of you an evil heart of unbelief in departing from the living God" (cf. "brethren"). Genuine believers can fall away.

Luke 8:13 says these believers fall away during a time of time of temptation. In Matthew's account, Jesus says, they *endure* only for a while. "For when tribulation or persecution arises because of the word, immediately he stumbles" (Mt. 13:21; see also Mk. 4:17). Their problem is when persecution comes because of the Word, instead of enduring, they fall away.

Constable observes that Jesus uses the phrase "fall away" of John the Baptist (Lk. 7:23). It is a different Greek word, but Constable says it has the same meaning. The Greek word translated "offended" in Luke 7:23 means, "to put a snare or stumbling block" in the way. Constable also uses Peter as an example of a genuine believer who renounced his faith because of persecution.

Dillow writes, "The issue in the parable is fruit bearing, not just salvation. The seed which fell on rocky soil produced growth, but the person in view fell away. But from what did he fall? There is not a word about heaven and hell in the parable. There is much about fruit bearing (Lk. 8:8) and progression to maturity (Lk. 8:14). The most plausible interpretation of the parable is simply to fall away from that progression which leads to maturity, to fruit bearing, and become a dead and carnal Christian. Adherents of perseverance may not like such an interpretation, but it is hardly fair to bring their theological exegesis to play and introduce notions of heaven and hell to which the parable never alludes" (Dillow, p. 399).

To sum up, virtually all commentaries contend that the people in parable of the sower who believed for a while were not genuine believers, because they only believed for a while, but the context indicates that those who believe are saved and, besides, it is possible for genuine believers to fall way.

JOHN 2:24

John 2 says, "Now when He was in Jerusalem at the Passover, during the feast, many believed in His name when they saw the signs which He did. But Jesus did not commit Himself to them, because He knew all *men*" (Jn. 2:23-24).

Jesus was in Jerusalem at the time of the Passover working miracles, probably miracles of healing. The blind were seeing, the deaf were hearing, the dumb were speaking, the lame were walking, and the crowds were watching with deep interest. These miracles were not spectacular displays to entertain; nor were they just miracles to heal individuals. They were *signs* to point to Christ. The people *saw* these signs (2:23). The Greek word translated "see" means, "to gaze, behold, contemplate, perceive, discern." Theirs was not a glance; it was a gaze. They stared and they contemplated. They got it.

Not Genuine Believers Some claim that although the text plainly says, "many believed in His name," they did not have true faith. Their faith was "superficial faith" (Tasker). Therefore, they were not genuine believers.

Martin Luther called this "milk faith". He adds, "This is faith of such as enthusiastically accede, and give in and believe that just as quickly withdraw when they hear something unpleasant or unexpected" (cited by Morris).

Calvin says that they had a "cold faith, which was only the shadow of faith." He calls it an "appearance of faith, which hitherto was fruitless, might ultimately be changed into true faith." He goes on to say, "Yet this was not a pretended faith by which they wished to gain reputation among men; for they were convinced that Christ was some great Prophet, and perhaps they even ascribed to him the honor of being the Messiah, of whom there was at that time a strong and general expectation. But as they did not understand the peculiar office of the Messiah, their faith was absurd, because it was exclusively directed to the world and earthly things. It was also a cold belief, and unaccompanied by the true feelings of the heart. For hypocrites assent to the Gospel, not that they may devote themselves in obedience to Christ, nor that with sincere piety they may follow Christ when he calls them, but because they do not venture to reject entirely the truth which they have known, and especially when they can find no reason for opposing it. For as they do not voluntarily, or of their own accord, make war with God, so when they perceive that his doctrine is opposed to their flesh and to their perverse desires, they are immediately offended, or at least withdraw from the faith which they had already embraced. When the Evangelist says, therefore, that those men *believed,* I do not understand that they counterfeited a faith which did not exist, but that they were in some way constrained to enroll themselves as the followers of Christ; and yet it appears that their faith was not true and genuine, because Christ excludes them from the number of those on whose sentiments reliance might be placed. Besides, that faith depended solely on miracles, and had no root in the Gospel, and therefore could not be steady or permanent. Miracles do indeed assist the children of God in arriving at the truth; but it does not amount to actual believing, when they admire the power of God so as merely to believe that it is true, but faith, let us know that there is a kind of faith which is perceived by the understanding only, and afterwards quickly disappears, because it is not fixed in the heart; and that is the faith which James calls *dead*; but true faith always depends on the Spirit of regeneration, (James 2:17, 20, 26). Observe that all do not derive equal profit from the works of God; for some are led by them to God, and others are only driven by a blind impulse, so that, while they perceive indeed the power of God, still they do not cease to wander in their own imaginations."

According to this notion, these people did not have real faith because their faith was based on miracles (2:23, Calvin, Godet) and because Jesus did not commit Himself to them (2:24, Calvin). Clarke states it clearly, "They believed him to be the promised Messiah, but did not believe in him to the salvation of their souls: for we find, from the following verse, that their hearts were not at all changed, because our blessed Lord could not trust himself to them."

Westcott thinks they recognized Him as the Messiah, "without any deeper trust (for the most part) in His Person (v. 24)." Bruce believes they were only "superficially impressed because they saw bare signs." According to him, they did not penetrate beneath the surface and grasp the truth that was signified by the sign. In commenting on this passage, Morris speaks of the "passing enthusiasms of men." He adds, "Many come to the point of decision. Yet we should probably not regard them as having a profound faith. They believe because they saw the 'signs'" and "it is not the deepest faith". He quotes R. H. Lightfoot who says this is "only a first attraction of the Lord (cf. 4:45, 48), and does not yet know Him as the Son of man, still less as a unique Son of God, and is therefore imperfect and liable to be overthrown".

Mitchell concisely states this interpretation when he says, "The people were intellectually persuaded that the things Jesus did were miracles, but their faith was not in the Person who performed those miracles. Because their faith was based on the spectacular (and Jesus knew this), it was not real." According to him and others, it was not saving faith.

Genuine Believers That conclusion is far from the mark. These people had real faith and were, therefore, genuine believers.

In the first place, the Greek text says, "they believed *into*," which scholars have argued is the strongest Greek construction for faith in the New Testament. Hodges calls it "a favorite expression in the Fourth Gospel for regenerating faith" (Hodges, *Bibliotheca Sacra*, vol. 135, pp. 140-153). Dillow says, "It is John's standard expression for saving faith" (Dillow, p. 105).

Furthermore, it also says they believed *in His name*, a phrase used elsewhere in the Gospel of John of genuine faith. It only appears three times in the Gospel of John and in both other places it describes genuine faith (cf. 1:12, 3:18). In fact, John 3:18 specifically says, "He who believes in Him is not condemned, but he who does not believe is condemned already, because he has not believed in the name of the only begotten Son of God." The reason they are condemned is that they do not believe in the name of the only begotten Son of God! Erickson says, "This construction ('believe in His name') has special significance to the Hebrews, who regarded one's name as virtually equivalent to the individual. Thus, to believe on or in the name of Jesus was to place one's personal trust in him" (Erickson, p. 940; he also says see *The Theology of the New Testament* by George Ladd, pp. 271-72).

Finally, Jesus performed miracles and John recorded them, so that people would believe and have eternal life (Jn. 20:30, 31). Jesus clearly said, "Believe Me that I am in the Father and the Father in Me, or else believe Me for the sake of the works themselves" (Jn. 14:11). Thomas is an illustration of someone who had to see before he would believe, He saw and believed (Jn. 20:24-29). Daniel Webster said, "I believe Jesus Christ to be the Son of God. The miracles which He wrought establish this in my mind."

Concerning this verse, *The NKJV Study Bible* states, "This was saving faith."

Untrustworthy Believers Even though these individuals had genuine faith that made them possessors of eternal life, Jesus did not believe in them. John says, "But Jesus did not commit Himself to them, because He knew all men, and had no need that anyone should testify of man, for He knew what was in man" (Jn. 2:24-25). The word translated "commit" in verse 24 is the same word that is translated "believe" in verse 23. They trusted in Him; He did not trust Himself to them. There is an obvious play on words in the Greek text. The reason Jesus did not trust Himself to this crowd of believers is because He knew all men. He did not have to be told what was inside of them. Jesus reads men's hearts like men read billboards.

Hodge suggests that the meaning of Jesus not committing Himself to them is that they did not have the courage of their convictions to confess Him before men. Consequentially, they were not His friends (Jn. 15:15. See the article by Hodge, *Bibliotheca Sacra*, vol. 135, pp. 140-153).

Govett says, "Our Lord did not trust these believers. Hence some have concluded that their faith was not real. But is everyone who really believes to the saving of his soul, trustworthy? Can you rest on him with explicit confidence, as one who will never deceive you, defraud you, never betray you? Alas, no! What says Paul? (1 Cor. vi. 8) 'Nay, you do wrong, and defraud, and that *your brethren.*' Could Jesus implicitly trust the twelve? Did they not all flee? Did not Peter cease and swear—'I know not the man?' The same class of persons is named began, in chap. xii. 42, 43. They believed, without confessing Christ. Are all who do not confess Christ, lost? Surely not! They will lose reward, because they own not Christ before man; they will be saved, because they believed."

To sum up, virtually all commentaries claim the people in Jerusalem, who believed in the name of Christ when they saw His miracles, were not genuine believers, because Jesus did not trust Himself to them, but the language that is used to describe their faith indicates that they were genuine believers. The fact that the Lord did not trust Himself to them simply means that He did not trust Himself to them as an intimate Friend, not that they were not saved.

ACTS 8:20

Luke records, "Then Simon himself also believed; and when he was baptized he continued with Philip, and was amazed, seeing the miracles and signs which were done. Now when the apostles who were at Jerusalem heard that Samaria had received the word of God, they sent Peter and John to them, who, when they had come down, prayed for them that they might receive the Holy Spirit. For as yet, He had fallen upon none of them. They had only been baptized in the name of the Lord Jesus. Then they laid hands on them, and they received the Holy Spirit. And when Simon saw that through the laying on of the apostles' hands the Holy Spirit was given, he offered them money, saying, 'Give me this power also, that anyone on whom I lay hands may receive the Holy Spirit.' But Peter said to him, 'Your money perish with you, because you thought that the gift of God could be purchased with money! You have neither part nor portion in this matter, for your heart is not right in the sight of God. Repent therefore of this your wickedness, and pray God if perhaps the thought of your heart may be forgiven you. For I see that you are poisoned by bitterness and bound by iniquity.' Then Simon answered and said, 'Pray to the Lord for me, that none of the things which you have spoken may come upon me'" (Acts 8:13-24).

Not A Genuine Believer Most commentators conclude that Simon was not saved. Acknowledging that Simon "had believed and been baptized; and apparently he continued faithful to Philip," Rackham says, "in spite of his baptism Simon had not really accepted *the word* or doctrine of the Messiah: and *his part and lot* in the kingdom was taken away, until he should repent." Rackham points out that post-New Testament writers branded Simon as the first founder of heresy and conclude that "it is extremely probable that Simon did not repent."

Alexander says Simon made a "false profession." He adds, "He professed belief, became a convert in the view of others, and in the customary way, by submitting to the rite of baptism." He then says, "As Simon had already been baptized (v. 13), the exhortation to repent might seem to have respect to this particular transgression [of wanting to buy the power to bestow the Holy Spirit], as a single act of disobedience. But the words of the Apostle show that the whole work or repentance and conversion were not yet to be performed."

Marshall notes that Simon believed, was baptized and clung to Philip. He then asks, "Was, then, Simon a genuine believer?" His answer is, "We need to read the rest of the story before we can evaluate his profession fairly," as if faith is not sufficient for salvation! Marshall interprets the phrase "no share in this matter" (8:21) as no share in the blessing of the gospel.

Bruce says, on the one hand, that the nature of Simon's faith must remain uncertain and, on the other hand, it was "superficial and inadequate." Gloag states that Simon "made a profession of faith in Jesus, and was baptized." Then, he writes, "That these impressions were temporary, that his heart was unchanged, the results soon showed." Later he adds, "Although it is said that Simon believed Philip, yet he can hardly be called a Christian at all—he was an outsider."

In his commentary on Acts, Calvin says, Simon did not give "himself over sincerely to Christ; for then his ambition, and that wicked and profane account which he made of the gifts of God, should not break out. And yet I am not of their mind who thinks that he made only a semblance of faith, seeing he did not believe. Luke says plainly that he believed, and the reason is added, because he was touched with wondering. How, then, doth he shortly after betray himself to be but a hypocrite? I answer, that there is some mean between faith and mere dissimulation. The Epicures [Epicureans] and Lucianists do profess that they believe, whereas notwithstanding they laugh inwardly, whereas the hope of eternal life is unto them a vain thing; finally, whereas they have no more godliness than dogs or swine. But there be many who howsoever they be not regenerate with the Spirit of adoption, and do not addict themselves unto God with the true affection of the heart, being overcome with the power of the Word, do not only confess that that is true which is taught, but are also touched with some fear of God, so that they receive doctrine; for they conceive that God must be heard; that he is both the author and also the judge of the world. Therefore, they make no semblance of faith before men, which is none, but they think that they believe. And this faith continues only for a time, whereof Christ speaks in Mark (Mark 4; Luke 8:13) to wit, when the seed of the Word conceived in the mind is, notwithstanding, choked forthwith with divers cares of the world, or with wicked affections, so that it never cometh to any ripeness; yea, rather, it grows out of kind unto unprofitable corn nothing worth. Such, therefore, was Simon's faith; he perceives that the doctrine of the gospel is true, and he is enforced to receive the same with the feeling of his conscience; but the groundwork is wanting; that is, the denial of himself. Whereupon it followed that his mind was enwrapped in dissimulation, which he utters forthwith. But let us know that his hypocrisy was such as he deceived himself in; and not that gross hypocrisy whereof Epicures and such like make boast; because they dare not confess the contempt of God." In other words, Simon had a faith that was not saving faith.

The reason commentators conclude that Simon did not have saving faith is because of what Peter says to him later. Calvin writes, "Simon Magus is said to have believed, though he soon after gave proof of his unbelief (Acts 8:13-18)" (Calvin, 3. II. 10). Ryrie states it clearly, when he writes, "Peter's denunciation in vv. 20-23 indicates that Simon's faith was not unto salvation (Jas. 2:14-20)" (*Ryrie Study Bible* on Acts 8:13). MacDonald says, "From what follows it seems that Simon had not been born again. He was a professor but not a possessor" (William McDonald, *Bible Believers Commentary*, p. 421).

A Genuine Believer Did Simon have saving faith? The text plainly says, "Simon himself also believed" (Acts 8:13). According to Luke, if a person believes, he is saved (Acts 16:30-31). That and that alone should settle the issue.

Moreover, Luke says, "Then Simon himself *also* believed" (Acts 8:13). Inglis, a nineteenth century author, wrote, "The word 'also' in the statement links Simon's faith with that of the Samaritans; and they, we read, 'believed Philip preaching the things concerning the kingdom of God, and the name of Jesus Christ.' And if you explain away that as other than saving faith, you make the Gospel itself of no effect and undermine the whole foundation of faith. Of what value are any of the promises to faith or any of the records of faith, if the testimony before us does not mean that Simon believed to the saving of his soul?" (Inglis, p. 52).

Philip thought Simon was saved. He baptized him! As Inglis points out, "Language could not be more explicit: 'Then Simon himself believed also: and when he was baptized, he continued with Philip, and wondered, beholding the miracles and signs which were done.'"

The NKJV Study Bible says, "Verse 13 indicates that Simon was a believer" (See note on Acts 8:18-25).

Bound Believers If Simon was a genuine believer, what is the explanation of Peter's strong language? Peter told Simon, "Your money perish with you, because you thought that the gift of God could be purchased with money!" (Acts 8:20). "For I see that you are poisoned by bitterness and bound by iniquity" (Acts 8:23).

Simon was in danger of perishing. The Greek noun translated "perish" means "destruction, waste, loss, perishing." It comes from a Greek verb that means, "to destroy, kill, lose utterly, perish," which is used *figuratively* of the loss of eternal life (A-S). Note, these words are not technical terms for eternal punishment. They can refer to either temporal or eternal destruction. They are used for everything from wasting oil (Mt. 26:8) to eternal perishing (Jn. 3:16). Therefore, the use of this word does not necessarily mean that Peter was threatening Simon with eternal damnation.

The question is, "Can 'perish' describe something that could happen to a believer?" The answer is, "Yes." Lang argues that out of the nearly 90 times the verb form of this noun is used, only 11 are clearly a reference to hell. It is used 33 times of the death of the body (Lang, cf. Mt. 2:13).

In the context of Acts 8, the perishing of money is temporal. Therefore, Simon's perishing is the temporal perishing of physical death (Dillow, pp. 327-28). Inglis observes, "If his money and he were to perish together, the word cannot be stretched beyond a temporal calamity" (Inglis, p. 48).

In Hebrews 11:39, this word unmistakably refers to the physical death of believers. The writer identifies himself with his readers (cf. "we") as those who draw back to perdition, that is, destruction, the same word that appears in Acts 8:20. Those who draw back are in danger of a premature physical death (1 Cor. 11:30). Hebrews 11:39 proves that *believers* (cf. "we") can "perish," but that does not mean they go to hell.

Paul says, "But those who desire to be rich fall into temptation and a snare, and *into* many foolish and harmful lusts which drown men in destruction and perdition" (1 Tim. 6:9). The context of this verse indicates that Paul is speaking about believers who fall into the temptation of a desire to be rich. The Greek word translated "destruction" comes from the verb "to destroy" and means "ruin, destruction, death." The one for "perdition" means, "destruction, waste, loss, perishing." It is used in Acts 8:20. It is generally assumed that the first of these words is a reference to the ruin of the body and the second to a loss of the soul in eternity (Hiebert, Gromacki). That is not necessarily the case. Perhaps, the second is "more intense" than the first (Kent). Both words are "probably" used "in the sense of ruin," suggesting "irretrievable loss" (Guthrie, see also, Hendriksen). Gromacki says, "destruction" involves "emotional and mental disorders, bankruptcy and family loss." He believes that "perdition" is a reference to the future life, but he says if it applies only to this life, then it is a "terrible waste of time and effort."

In Luke 13, some told Jesus about "the Galileans whose blood Pilate had mingled with their sacrifices" (Lk. 13:1). Jesus replied, "Do you suppose that these Galileans were worse sinners than all *other* Galileans, because they suffered such things? I tell you, no; but unless you repent you will all likewise perish" (Lk. 13:2-3). Notice, the Galileans suffered physical death and Jesus said that those who did not repent would *likewise perish*. The implication of that phrase seems to be that they would suffer physical death.

Part of Jesus' reply was a parable concerning a fig tree (Lk. 13:6-9). The parable is a continuation of the previous warning to repent (Plummer). It fits "exceptionally well" with what has just been said (Geldenhuys). It is common for commentators to conclude that the fig tree represents Israel (Godet, Creed, Geldenhuys) and that it is predicting physical death. Barclay says, "But Jesus went on to say that if his hearers did not repent they too would perish. What did he mean? One thing is clear—he foresaw and foretold the destruction of Jerusalem, which happened in A.D. 70 (cf. Luke 21:21–24). He knew well that if the Jews went on with their intrigues, their rebellions, their plottings, their political ambitions, they were simply going to commit national suicide; he knew that in the end Rome would step in and obliterate the nation; and that is precisely what happened." In other words, "perish," in Luke 13:3, the verb form of the noun used in Acts 8:20, means physical death.

Simon was bitter and in the bond of iniquity. Believers can be bitter (Eph. 4:31) and be bound by sin (Rom. 6:12, 7:23). Inglis makes the interesting observation that the bitterness and bond of iniquity "describes not the state in which Simon committed the sin, but the mood in which he received the rebuke; for 'bitterness' elsewhere evidently means irritation or displeasure, and the gall of bitterness would signify the heat of displeasure which brought the scowl upon his countenance, and showed that the influence under which he had sinned was not yet dissolved" (Inglis, p. 52).

Dillow explains Simon's sin. "What was Simon's sin? It was selfish ambition. 'Give this authority to me as well, so that everyone on whom I lay my hands may receive the Holy Spirit.' Peter concluded that Simon wanted to purchase the power to pass on the gift of the Holy Spirit and that his heart was not right with God. Surely the presence of prideful ambition is not a basis for concluding that a man is not saved! Who among us has not at one time or another been tempted in this way? Unholy rivalries and ambitions often plague relationships between true Christians. To say the presence of this sin invalidates the claim to regeneration is unrealistic" (Dillow, p. 327).

To sum up, virtually all commentaries conclude that Simon's sin proves that he was not a genuine believer, but the text plainly says that he believed. Believers are capable of doing what Simon did (wanting to pay for a spiritual privilege) and his possible perishing is temporal, not eternal. Terms such as "gall of bitterness," "bond of iniquity" and "perish" are strong words, but not necessarily inconsistent with being a believer.

Summary: It is common for commentaries to conclude that when the New Testament says some people believed that they had a false faith, because of something that is said about them after they believed, but it can be demonstrated that they are people who had real faith.

Several conclusions can be drawn from this study. First, there is no such thing as a false faith *in the New Testament*. That does not mean that what some people call faith today is real New Testament faith.

At the same time, this is more than an exegetical or theological issue. It is an intensely practical issue, because, based on this approach to the New Testament, some teach that people must look at their life after trusting Christ to make sure they had real faith. That is dangerous. The test of real faith is not the results it produces in one's life. It is the *content* of the faith itself. The explanation of a person who is not walking with the Lord may not be anything more than that individual is a believer out of the will of God.

Those who genuinely trust Jesus Christ for the gift of eternal life can fall away, not enter a life of intimate fellowship with the Lord, be misguided and even be bitter and in the bond of sin. Believers can fall; their faith cannot fail. Unfortunately, some genuine Christians can and do live carnal lives (1 Cor. 3:1-4).

10
EXAMINE YOURSELF
FOR ASSURANCE

Lordship Salvation theology teaches that there is a real faith and a false faith and the way to determine the difference is that real faith always results in behavioral change that endures, whereas false faith does not. Therefore, to determine if you are saved, you should examine yourself (2 Cor. 13:5). You should make your calling an election sure (2 Pet. 1:10). In other words, works are the basis of assurance of salvation. The book of 1 John is said to contain tests of eternal life.

For example, MacArthur wrote, "Genuine assurance comes from seeing the Holy Spirit's transforming work in one's life, not from clinging to the memory of some experience" (MacArthur, GAJ, p. 23).

2 Corinthians 13:5

Paul says, "Examine yorurselves as to whether you are in the faith. Prove your own selves. Do you not know yourselves, that Jesus Christ is in you?—unless you are disqualified. But I trust that you will know that we are not disqualified" (2 Cor. 13:5-6). They were seeking proof that Christ was speaking in Paul (2 Cor. 12:3). Now Paul tells them to examine themselves. The exam is to see whether or not they are "in the faith."

The Lordship Salvation View The Lordship explanation of 2 Corinthians 13:6 is that "in the faith" means, being in Christ, that is, being saved. MacArthur uses this verse to suggest that people should examine themselves to see if they are genuine believers or if the had counterfeit faith (MacArthur, FW, p. 141).

The Meaning of 2 Corinthians 13:5 Is Paul questioning whether or not they are believers? Plummer remarks that it is difficult to understand how he could tell them to test themselves as to whether they are in the faith after having said "by faith you stand" (cf. 2 Cor. 1:24). He concludes Paul wrote this passage first! Indeed Paul does assume throughout the book that the Corinthians were genuine believers. The book is addressed "to the church of God which is at Corinth with all the saints who are in all Achaia" (2 Cor. 1:1). He calls them "beloved" (2 Cor. 7:1) and "brethren" (2 Cor. 8:1). He refers to them as his spiritual children (2 Cor. 12:14), but beyond those specific references the whole tenor of the book is that it is addressed to believers exhorting them to Christian living. It is highly unlikely, if not odd, that he would question their salvation at the end of the book.

The issue is "What is the meaning of the phrase 'in the faith.'?" Elsewhere, Paul uses the phrase "not of one being justified or regenerated, but of one operating within the confines of Christian conviction (cf. 1 Cor. 16:13, Titus 1:13)." (Hodges, AF, pp. 200-201).

Paul asks, "Do you not know yourselves that Jesus Christ is in you?" (2 Cor. 13:5). The Greek text indicates that Paul expected an affirmative answer. The question is, what is it Paul was sure they knew? What does he mean by "Jesus Christ is in you?" In this context that phrase seems to mean Christ was working in and even through them. They were seeking a proof of Christ speaking in Paul (2 Cor. 12:3). Paul says examine yourselves to see if Christ is speaking in you.

Hodges says the idea that they were abandoned to everlasting perdition is "obviously not the sense here" (Hodges, AF, p. 306). That is clearly true, for in the next verse Paul says, "But I trust that you will know that we are not disqualified" (2 Cor. 13:6). In speaking of his own disqualification did Paul mean to imply that he could not be a genuine believer? That is not even remotely the issue in this passage. The issue is whether or not Christ was speaking in Paul (2 Cor. 13:3). What was possible is that Christ was not speaking in Paul or in them! In 1 Corinthians 9:27 Paul uses the word "disqualified" of his service, not his salvation.

In his book, *Once Saved, Always Saved*, R. T. Kendall, the former Pastor of Westminster Chapel in London, says, "In 2 Corinthians 13:5-7 Paul takes up with them the question of accreditation and expresses himself to the effect that it matters little to them whether he himself seems to be 'approved' so long as they show themselves approved by Jesus Christ being manifest in them. Paul is not turning on them at the last moment and raising the question of whether or not they were even saved (how often people quote 2 Corinthians 13:5 out of context); he challenges them to prove his own worth in light of his apostleship being questioned. The Greek does not read, 'Examine yourselves to see if you are in the faith'; it is rather, "examine yourselves if you are in the faith." As they were seeking a proof of Christ speaking through Paul (2 Corinthians 13:3), Paul turns on them and asks them to prove that Christ is speaking through them. Thus, he says that Jesus Christ is speaking in them unless they have failed the test (2 Corinthians 5). The contrast is not that of being saved or lost, but whether or not, as saved people, Christ is openly manifest in them. This kind of testing is not exactly the same thing as being 'tried by fire.' At the Judgment Seat of Christ although the notion of being proved by testing is not completely unrelated there is a certain test that will prove whether or not Christ is speaking through us. The test does not await the Judgment Seat of Christ, but one cannot but notice how important it is to be so utterly yielded to the Lord that we know that he is speaking through us. It is this kind of obedience that will be tried on the last day" (Kendall, p. 174).

2 Peter 1:10

Peter exhorts, "Therefore brethren, be even more diligent to make your calling and election sure" (2 Pet. 1:10). Believers (cf. "brethren") are to be diligent to make their calling and election sure.

The Lordship Salvation View The Lordship Salvation explanation of 2 Peter 1:10 is that believers are to examine their lives to see if they are saved. MacArthur uses 2 Peter 1:10 to teach that people should examine themselves to see if they are genuine believers or if they had counterfeit faith (MacArthur, FW, p. 141).

The Meaning of 2 Peter 1:10 The issue is the meaning of the word "sure." Mayor says it means, to "certify," "confirm," "attest." The same word is used in 2 Peter 1:19 where it is rendered "confirmed." In that verse, Peter is saying the transfiguration demonstrated, confirmed the prophetic word to others. Does 2 Peter 1:19 mean that the prophetic word was not sure before the transfiguration? Absurd! The verb form of this noun is translated "confirm" (Heb. 2:3) and "establish" (1 Cor. 1:6, Col. 2:7, Heb. 13:9). In other words, believers are to add Christian traits to their faith and validate thier choosing and calling to others.

Hodges says, "When a Christian develops the character qualities of vv 5-7, he is producing valid evidence for others to observe that God has indeed 'called' and 'chosen' him. This is similar to James's doctrine of justification by works before men. The unsaved are not likely to believe that we are in God's favor on our own say-so alone. But a life filled with moral virtue and capped with love (v 7) can be very persuasive. As the Lord Jesus put it: 'By this all will know that you are my disciples, if you have love for one another' (John 13:35)" (Hodges, unpublished class notes on 2 Peter).

It should also be pointed out that Hodges believes that the calling and election are not to salvation, but a call to service. He bases his view on the fact that the phrase "calling and election" is in the reverse order from our calling to salvation (Rom. 8:30) and that the order that appears in 2 Peter 1:10 is used by Jesus to refer to service (Mt.

20:16, 22:14). He says, "We propose, therefore, that Peter's words do not refer here to a pre-temporal election to eternal salvation, which by its very nature would precede the call to salvation. Instead, all Christians have been given a 'royal' summons by God Himself, 'who calls [us] into His own kingdom and glory' (1 Thess 2:12). And a supremely significant part of that glory is the privilege of co-reigning with Christ (2 Tim 2:12; Rev 2:26-27; 3:21). But not all Christians are chosen to co-reign! Paul writes: 'If we endure, we shall also reign with Him' (2 Tim 2:12, italics added); and he also wrote, 'and *joint heirs* with Christ, if indeed we suffer with Him, that we may also be glorified together' (Rom 8:17b, italics added)."

1 JOHN

The Lordship Salvation View The Lordship Salvation interpretation of 1 John is that it gives a list of tests of eternal life so that people can have assurance of salvation. For example, MacArthur says, 1 John was written "to deal with precisely the issue of assurance" (MacArthur, FW, p. 166). In his book on the assurance of salvation entitled *Saved Without a Doubt*, John MacArthur claims 1 John contains a series of eleven tests to determine whether or not people possess eternal life (See MacArthur, SWD, pp. 67-91).

1. Have you enjoyed fellowship with Christ and the Father? (1 Jn. 1:2-3)
2. Are you sensitive to sin? (1 Jn. 1:5-10)
3. Do you obey God's word? (1 Jn. 2:3)
4. Do you reject this evil world? (1 Jn. 2:15)
5. Do you eagerly await Christ's Return? (1 Jn. 3:2-3)
6. Do you see a decreasing pattern of sin in your life? (1 Jn. 3:4-10)
7. Do you love other Christians? (1 Jn. 3:10)

8. Do you experience answered prayer? (1 Jn. 3:22)
9. Do you experience the ministry of the Holy Spirit?
   (1 Jn. 4:13)
10. Do you discern between spiritual truth and error?
    (1 Jn. 4:1-3)
11. Have you suffered rejection because of your faith?
    (1 Jn. 3:13)

The Purpose of 1 John The purpose of 1 John is not to give tests to see if someone is saved. There is no doubt in the author's mind that the people to whom he is writing are genuine believers. What could possibly be clearer than, 'I write to you, little children, because your sins are forgiven you for His name's sake" (1 Jn. 2:12).

The purpose of 1 John is fellowship (1 Jn. 1:3). In his discussion of the plan of the epistle, Westcott says 'The thought of a fellowship between God and man, made possible and in part realized in a Christian church, runs through the whole epistle" (Westcott, p. xlvii). In his commentary on 1 John, Hodges says John writes, "to sustain and promote fellowship with God in the face of the theological errors that constitute an attack on this fellowship" (Hodges, *The Epistles of John*, p. 34).

Summary: The New Testament does not teach that the basis of assurance is the works produced in one's life. The basis of assurance is faith in God's promise that all who trust Christ are given eternal life.

Lordship Salvation teaches that works are the basis of assurance of salvation. Most within the movement would say that works are the *only* basis of assurance. MacArthur once emphatically declared, "The only validation of salvation is a life of obedience. It is the only possible proof that a person really knows Jesus Christ. If one does not obey Christ as a pattern of life, then professing to know Him is an empty verbal exercise" (MacArthur, GAJ, p. 194). Notice the word "only." MacArthur approvingly quotes Jonathan Edwards, who said,

"It is not God's design that men should obtain assurance in any other way than by mortifying, increasing in grace and obtaining the lively exercise of it" (MacArthur, GAJ, p. 231). Notice the phrase "any other way."

Apparently, MacArthur has changed his position on the assurance of salvation. In his book, *Saved Without a Doubt,* he makes a distinction between objective assurance and subjective assurance. Concerning objective assurance, he writes, "We're to be assured of our salvation first and foremost because Scripture promises eternal life to those who believe in Christ (John 20:31). God's Word and the guarantee of life to believers is thus the foundation of all assurance." According to MacArthur, subjective assurance is "the fruit of righteousness in the believer's life and the internal witness of the Spirit" (MacArthur, SWD, p. 11). His book puts virtually all the focus on subjective assurance, but he, at least, acknowledges that first we can be assured of salvation because the Scripture promises eternal life to all who believe.

Actually, the logical conclusion of the Lordship Salvation position is that no one can know for sure they are saved. Think about it. If all believers always produce works, if all believers endure to the end and if those works and endurance are the basis of assurance, people can never be sure that they are saved, because they have not endured to the end yet.

To put this in perspective, let me ask, "Is it possible to have the assurance of salvation the day one gets saved?" I once got into a long discussion with a man defending Lordship Salvation. At one point I said to him, "If you and I lead a man to Christ tonight, could that individual go home and lay his head on his pillow and know that he had eternal life?" Without batting an eye, he replied, "No." My response to him was, "At least you are consistent."

Years ago, I had lunch with a theology professor, who believed that believers would preserve to the end. I asked him if he knew for sure he was going to heaven. His answer was something to the effect that he had met all the conditions for salvation. When I pressed him for a more specific answer, all he would ever say was that there was evidence that God was working in his life! He would never say that he knew for sure he was going to heaven, because he knew that was logically impossible given his theology.

Telling people to examine their life to make sure they are saved produces confusion over the terms of salvation, doubts over the assurance of salvation and a judgmental attitude over the consequences of salvation. Remember Berkhof, a Reformed theologian, wrote that the outcome of making works the basis of assurance "tended to lead to ever-increasing doubt, confusion, and uncertainty" (Berkhof, p. 508).

If the Lordship Salvation view is right that works are the primary basis of assurance, how much is enough? The usual answer is that to have assurance, people must see a pattern of holiness in their lives. That really does not answer the question. How much holiness is enough to satisfy that requirement? What percentage of a person's life must manifest this pattern? Furthermore, even if there is a "pattern," how can one know that it is real rather than self-deception? Is one to take another's estimation of holiness as the ground for assurance? Do I take my own evaluation? If assurance rests on following a pattern of holiness, is it not highly probable that the motive for doing good works may become self-centered and not God-centered?

A young man I had met, but I did not know well, came to see me. I knew his parents—very well. They were outstanding Christians who had faithfully served the Lord all of their lives. The father of the young man was particularly knowledgeable concerning the Scripture. So, I knew the fellow had been reared in a Christian home. As we began to talk this young man gave a clear testimony that he had trusted Christ years ago. He told me that for the past nine months, he had attended a well-known evangelical church. The pastor was known far and wide as a proclaimer of Lordship Salvation. The fellow in my office proceeded to tell me that after listening to that Bible teacher for nine months, he concluded he was not saved! After talking with the him at length and in detail, there was no doubt in my mind, nor his, that he truly had been saved years before, but listening to Lordship Salvation preached week after week had made this sensitive, introspective fellow doubt his salvation to the point that he wanted to just give up. That is sad!

Lordship Salvation produces confusion and doubt, even for those well established in the faith. MacArthur begins his book on assurance with a letter he received from a man in his own church. The letter reads, "I've been attending Grace Church for several years. As a result of a growing conviction in my heart, your preaching, and my seeming powerlessness against the temptations which arise in my heart and which I constantly succumb to, my growing doubts have led me to believe that I'm not saved. How sad it is, John, for me not to be able to enter in because of the sin which clings to me and from which I long to be free. How bizarre for one who has had advanced biblical training and who teaches in Sunday School with heartfelt conviction! So many times I have determined in my heart to repent, to shake loose my desire to sin, to forsake all for Jesus, only to find myself doing the sin I don't want to do and not doing the good I want to do. After my fiancée and I broke up, I memorized Ephesians as part of an all-out effort against sin, only to find myself weaker and more painfully aware of my sinfulness, more prone to sin than ever before, and grabbing cheap thrills to push back the pain of lost love. This occurs mostly in the heart, John, but that's where it counts and that's where we live. I sin because I'm a sinner. I'm like a soldier without armor running across a battlefield getting shot up by fiery darts from the enemy. I couldn't leave the church if I wanted to. I love the people, and I'm enthralled by the Gospel of the beautiful Messiah. But I'm a pile of manure on the white marble floor of Christ, a mongrel dog that sneaked in the back door of the king's banquet to lick the crumbs off the floor, and being close to Christians who are rich in the blessings of Christ, I get some of the overflow and ask you to pray for me as you think best" (MacArthur, SWD, p. 7-8).

The Bible declares that those who believe *have* (present tense) eternal life and they can know it now (1 Jn. 5:13). The Lordship Salvation teaching concerning assurance produces confusion, doubt and sometimes worse! Whom will you believe? Some preacher, who would point you to your works, or the Word of God that points you to the Work of Christ?

Be sure that you can be absolutely sure.

11
A HISTORICAL PERSPECTVE

If the Bible teaches that assurance in based on faith, how did anyone ever get the idea that assurance is based on works? Who started the notion that in order to be certain of salvation people should look at themselves and not Christ and/or the cross? A brief survey of the issue of assurance of salvation in church history will put this issue into perspective.

A short version of what happened can be found in Berkhof's theology. After the Reformers passed off the scene, a group, who became known as the Puritans, separated saving faith and assurance, putting the emphasis more and more on an examination of one's works as the basis of assurance. Berkhof says that the Canons of Dort teach that assurance "springs from faith in God's promises, from the testimony of the Holy Spirit, and from the exercise of a good conscience and doing good works, and is enjoyed according to the measure of faith" (Berkhof, p. 507). Notice, that while faith in God's promises is included, so are a number of other things. The shift away from faith including assurance had begun. The Synod of Dort was held in 1618-1619.

Berkhof says that the Westminster Confession, while speaking of the full assurance of faith, "asserts that this does not so belong to the essence of faith that a true believer may have to wait for a long time in," which caused some theologians to deny that personal assurance belongs to the essence of faith" (Berkhof, p. 508). The separation of faith and assurance is now complete. The Westminster Confession of Faith was adopted in England in 1648.

According to Berkhof, "pietistic Nomism asserts that assurance does not belong to the very being, but only to the well-being of faith" (Berkhof, p. 508). He adds that according to this view, assurance can be secured "only by continuous and conscientious introspection. All kinds of 'marks of the spiritual life,' derived not from Scripture but from the lives of approved Christians, became the standard of self-examination. The outcome proved, however, that this method was not calculated to produce assurance, but tended to lead to ever-increasing doubt, confusion, and uncertainty" (Berkhof, p. 508).

A more detailed description of what happened is given by Kendall. In 1976, R. T. Kendall wrote a Ph. D. dissertation at Oxford University later published under the title *Calvin and English Calvinism to 1649*. The thesis of this book is that the doctrine of salvation, specifically the doctrine of saving faith and assurance in the Westminster Confession of 1648, is more the legacy of the Puritan William Perkins, than the Reformer John Calvin. What follows is a simplified summary of that involved and sometimes complex thesis.

John Calvin

John Calvin (1509-64) believed in double predestination, that is, God ordained some to salvation and some to damnation. According to Kendall, Calvin himself also believed that Christ died for all men, not just the elect (cf. Calvin's commentary on Isa. 53:12, Mk. 14:24, Jn. 1:29, Rom. 5:15, Gal. 5:12, Heb. 9:28). Calvin wrote a point-by-point refutation of the Council of Trent and when he came to the statement that Christ died for all men he stated that he had no comment.

For Calvin, salvation is by faith in Christ. He describes faith as "illumination," "firm conviction," "assurance," "full assurance." It is intellectual and passive. Faith is man being fully persuaded in his mind.

Calvin also taught that an unbeliever could have "temporary faith" (cf. Lk. 8:13, Heb. 6:4-5). Saving faith in the elect is indestructible, but Calvin did not go to the next step as those after him did and conclude that assurance was based on works produced by faith. "We shall not find assurance of our election in ourselves," Calvin wrote (*Institutes*, vol. 3, XXIV, 5). Kendall declares, "He (Calvin) thinks Christ's death is a sufficient pledge and merely seeing Him is assuring. Never does he employ 2 Peter 1:10 in connection with seeking assurance of salvation" (Kendall, p. 125). "Calvin constantly urges men not to look to themselves" (Kendall, p. 25). If we want to know we're in the number of the elect, we must be persuaded that Christ died for us" (Kendall, p. 28).

Theodore Beza

Calvin's successor in Geneva was Theodore Beza (1519-1605). While he, like Calvin before him, believed in double predestination, unlike Calvin Beza believed in limited atonement. Kendall argues that Beza's doctrine of limited atonement: "1) inhibits the believer from looking directly to Christ's death for assurance, 2) precipitates an implicit distinction between faith and assurance, 3) tends to put repentance before faith in the *ordo salutis*, and then 4) plants the seeds of voluntarism in the doctrine of faith" (Kendall, p. 29). "Voluntarism is the view that faith is an act of will in contrast to a passive persuasion in the mind" (Kendall, p. 3).

Note carefully, if Christ died only for the elect and did not die for everyone, the issue becomes, "How do I know that I am one of the elect for whom Christ died?" I can no longer say, "I know Christ died for me because He died for all and I am trusting in what He did and therefore I can know I'm saved."

Kendall put it like this: "We have no pledge, as it were, that we are elect for we have no way of knowing whether we are one of those for whom Christ died. Had Christ died for all we could freely know we are elected, but Beza has told us Christ died for the elect. This makes trusting Christ presumptuous, if not dangerous: We could be putting our trust in one who did not die for us and therefore be damned. Thus, we can no more trust Christ's death by a direct act of faith than we can infallibly project that we are among the number chosen for eternity: for the number of the elect and the number for whom Christ died are one and the same. The ground of assurance, then, must be sought elsewhere than in Christ" (Kendall, p. 32).

For Beza, sanctification or good works is the infallible proof of saving faith. In his little catechism he asks, "But whereby may a man know whether he has faith or not? Answer: by good works." Calvin thought that looking to ourselves would lead to anxiety or sure damnation. Not Beza. Kendall concludes that it is as though Beza says all who have the affects have faith; I have the affects, therefore, I have faith. Assurance of salvation, then, is not based on Scripture but on a syllogism, not on looking to Christ but on logic.

Kendall summed it up when he said, "For what Beza does not do is point men to Christ; he points men instead to faith. If they conclude that they have faith, then they may conclude that they have Christ. To Calvin, looking to Christ is faith; Calvin could point men directly to Christ since Christ died for all. Beza begins not with Christ but with faith; faith, if found, is rewarded with salvation in Christ but this salvation comes to the believer indirectly" (Kendall, p. 34). Beza depicts conversion as a composite of two works of grace: 'First grace' (faith) and a 'second grace' (sanctification). The first grace is rendered void, however, if it is not ratified by the second. It is the second grace which assures, for the first grace may not persevere (Kendall, p. 35).

Since Beza makes sanctification the ground of assurance, it is not surprising that he appeals to 2 Peter 1:10 in connection with the assurance of election, something Calvin did not do. As Kendall says, "When Christ is not held forth to all men as the immediate ground of assurance, the result is not only introspection on our part but a need to assure ourselves upon the very grounds Calvin warns against" (Kendall, p. 38).

William Perkins

In 1589, William Perkins (1558-1602) published his first major work entitled *A Treatise Tending Unto A Declaration Whether A Man May Be In The Estate Of Damnation Or In The Estate Of Grace: And If He Be In the First How He May In Time Come Out of It: Given The Second How He May Discern It And Persevere In The Same To The End* (titles were long in those days!). By the end of the sixteenth century, he had replaced Calvin and Beza as the most popular author of religious works in England. Though he always saw himself in the mainstream of the Church of England, he has been called "the greatest of the sixteenth century Puritan theologians" and the "prince of the theologians" (Kendall, p. 53). Perkins, like Calvin and Beza before him, believed in double predestination but he devoted himself to showing men how they could make their calling and election sure to themselves. He was the fountainhead of the concept that, based on 2 Peter 1:10, we can prove to ourselves that election is by our works. He was not the first to suggest this idea. He was the one who synthesized the system and popularized it.

In his work, *A Treatise on whether a Man may be in the estate of Damnation or in the Estate of Grace*, Perkins begins by describing the reprobate, that is, the unregenerate. According to Perkins, an unbeliever may profess to believe the gospel, he may be given a taste of God's goodness, which issues in a change of behavior, he may be often so like Christians that none but Christ can discern the true Christian from the apparent Christian and by the gift of prophecy he may be able to interpret and expound the Scripture. A reprobate may be in the visible church, obey it in word and deed and be taken for a member of Christ. How, then, does a person know he is a true Christian?

Perkins' sole advice for the doubting Christian is embodied in 2 Peter 1:10 and according to him that verse means nothing else but to practice the virtues of the moral law. He makes the change of life the ground of assurance! But if the reprobate can experience a change of behavior, how does a person know he is not a reprobate?

Kendall, whose original Ph.D. dissertation at Oxford was entitled *The Nature of Saving Faith Of William Perkins To The Westminster Assembly* concluded: "The central question to which Perkins devoted himself is the one he never satisfactorily answers: how a man 'maie discerne' he is in the state of grace. Beza's doctrine of limited atonement and Calvin's doctrine of temporary faith are the two main ingredients that flavor Perkins' thinking in this connection; but these ingredients do not mix well, and can hardly be digested into a system that revolves around the premise that sanctification is the ground of assurance. Perkins' kind of assurance is not an improvement over the reprobate's persuasion 'for the time in which he feeleth it.' Perkins' system literally requires a 'descending into our owne hearts,' the introspection Calvin warns against. The teachings of limited atonement are preponderantly the doctrine which forfeits faith as assurance in Perkins' thought. Since there is no way, apart from extraordinary revelation, that one can know that he was one of those for whom Christ died, one must *do* certain things and infer His assurance. . . . Believing in Christ to Perkins means sooner or later to descend inside oneself; the eventual result is not merely introspection, but a doctrine of faith that could easily breed legalism. The doing of good works, while not the ground of faith, is the ground of assurance. The apostle's admonition in 2 Peter 1:10 is the Spirit's charge that 'by keeping a continual course in good works' we may have 'the most evident tokens of election'" (Kendall, pp. 74-75).

A contemporary reported that Perkins died in the conflict of a troubled conscience. No wonder!

Perkins' legacy, based more on Beza than Calvin, ended up in the Westminster Confession of Faith.

Jacobus Arminius

Jacobus Arminius (about 1559-1609) studied under Beza in Geneva. In 1587, he became a pastor in Amsterdam. In 1591, he was asked to defend Beza's doctrine of predestination because of a pamphlet circulating against it. Instead of defending Beza, Arminius agreed with the pamphlet! Arminius was an admirer of Perkins, but when Perkins' treatise on predestination appeared in Holland he prepared an answer to it but did not publish it (about 1602). From 1603-1609, when he died, Arminius was professor of theology at Leiden. Those six years were marked by intense controversy almost entirely concerning predestination.

Arminius differed with the Calvinists in that he believed that God decreed to save those He knew from all eternity would believe and persevere. He further believed that faith was a gift of God and that it is "impossible for believers as long as they remain believers to decline from salvation" (*The Works of Arminius*, vol. 2, p. 677 ff.).

Both the predestinarians and Arminius are agreed: Those who reject the gospel or apostatize are reprobates. The predestinarians teach that believers persevere because they were elected; Arminius says God elects believers whom He foresees will persevere. The predestinarians retreat to their doctrine of temporary faith. Arminius simply says faith can fail. There is no practical difference between the two schools of thought. If believers do not persevere they are not saved.

The Remonstrance

In 1610, the year after Arminius' death, his followers summarized his position in the now famous remonstrance (that is, a strong or formal protest). Kendall summarizes those five articles: "1) God has decreed Jesus Christ as the redeemer of men and decreed to save all who believe on Him; 2) Christ died for all but only believers enjoy forgiveness of sins; 3) man must be regenerated by the spirit; 4) grace is 'not irresistible'; and 5) perseverance is granted 'through the assistance of the grace of the Holy Spirit' but whether one can fall from 'life in Christ' is left open" (Kendall, pp. 149-150).

The Canons of Dort

On May 29, 1619, the Senate of Dordrecht (commonly called the Synod of Dort; Dordrecht or Dort is a city is Southern Netherlands) issued five canons to counter the five articles. Those now very famous five canons can be summarized as follows: "1) That God's eternal decree of predestination is the cause of election and reprobation and that this decree is not based on foreseen faith; 2) that Christ died for the elect only; 3) and (4) that men by nature are unable to seek God apart from the spirit and that grace is irresistible; and 5) the elect will surely persevere in faith to the end" (Kendall, p. 150). The popular summary of the Canons of Dort follows the letters of Tulip: Total depravity, Unconditional election, Limited atonement, Irresistible grace and Perseverance of the saints.

The Senate of Dort also declared that men may have assurance of election by observing in themselves the infallible fruits of election, but those who lack this "assured confidence" must not necessarily rank themselves among the reprobates if they seriously desire to please God. Kendall observes, "The Senate of Dort represents a substantial departure from Calvin's doctrine of faith. Moreover, Perkins' idea of the least measure of faith, the will to believe, is given creedal sanction at Dort" (Kendall, p. 150).

William Ames

William Ames (1576-1633) reportedly exercised enormous power behind the scenes at the Senate of Dort. Like those before him, he believed in double predestination. He even wrote the preface for a defense of supralapsarianism. The words infralapsarianism and sublapsarianism apparently were words that were not used before the Senate of Dort. They appear shortly thereafter. The word lapsarian simply refers to one who believes that man has fallen. The theological controversy over lapsarianism, however, concerns the subject of election. Hypercalvinists are supralapsarian, that is, they believe that the decree to elect and reprobate was before the decree to permit the fall. Sublapsarians teach that the decree to elect was after the decree to permit the fall. Sublapsarians of necessity believe in limited atonement. Infralapsarianism is the position that the decree to elect was not only after the decree to permit the fall, but also the decree to provide salvation. This view allows for an unlimited atonement. This is the view of moderate Calvinists and Arminians. The Arminians, however, go one step further and define the election as based on foreseen faith.

Williams Ames was William Perkins' most famous disciple. Ames retained Perkins' double predestination doctrine, but he saw the incompatibility of making works the ground of assurance while also espousing the doctrine of temporary faith. In his system, there is no hint that a person could imagine that his sanctification was but a temporary faith. In the words of Kendall, "Ames has taken the voluntarism that was begun in Beza's theology and popularized by Perkins, and brings it into a logical conclusion. Man is thus seen earning God's grace by a willingness to consecrate himself to a godly life. The irony is that this theology purports the lie in a thoroughly predestinarian system" (Kendall, pp. 162-63). Kendall concluded his discussion of Ames by saying, "If ever a man deserved the name of 'Puritan' it is William Ames. Apart from his keen interest in ecclesiological matters, his soteriology alone which preeminently stresses purity of life bears out all that this word has implied. Indeed, considering the stature he had in the Massachusetts Bay, whose early residents gave America her soul, much of what became identified with the legalism and the stringency of the early New England way is to be imputed largely to William Ames" (Kendall, p. 164).

John Cotton

John Cotton (1584-1652) was the first major figure within the predestinarian family to depart from the prevailing view. Cotton believed in predestination. He even believed that man was as passive in his regeneration as in his first generation. Nevertheless, he also later in his ministry concluded that faith alone is the evidence of justification and sanctification is no proof of justification. He believed that by virtue of temporary faith, the reprobate may produce a "real" sanctification and that conversely sanctification may be less discernible on true saints than in some hypocrites. He came to the place where he refused to teach that sanctification proved one's election. He particularly rejected the then popular use of 2 Peter 1:10 as a proof text for sanctification being the basis of assurance appealing to Calvin's view of that verse for support. For Cotton, the witness of the Spirit was sufficient to give full assurance.

Westminister Confession of Faith

In 1643, the British parliament commissioned the Westminster Assembly, composed of 151 English Puritans. Between 1643 and 1649, the group held 1,163 daily sessions. They drew up a directory of public worship (1644), a document on the form of government which was Presbyterian (1645), and the famous creed called the Westminster Confession of Faith (1646). Then, they produced the longer and shorter catechisms (Cairns, pp. 340-341).

Kendall points out that the Westminster Assembly drew up a document that spoke directly against men of the day who taught things like: the apostles not only appropriated assurance, they even appropriated full assurance to faith alone and sanctification was not the grounds of assurance (Kendall, pp. 184-89). Furthermore, 2 Peter 1:10, the very verse through which Perkins and his followers primarily appealed as the formula for obtaining personal assurance of election, appears in the confession as teaching the basis for assurance. On top of that, Kendall says, "While the Westminster divines never intended to make works the ground of salvation, they could hardly have come closer since saving faith is defined as 'yeelding obedience' to God's commands, the 'principall acts' of faith *being of the will*, this seems to make the claim 'free grace' suspect" (Kendall, p. 205).

Kendall's Conclusion

Kendall concludes his dissertation by making several observations: "The question of perseverance remains. At first glance, Westminster theology seems to have polarized itself against the Arminian hypothesis that the regenerate can fall but not so; by taking back assurance from those who fall grievously into sin, the subject becomes suspect—both in his own eyes and in the eyes of others—in that he is back to zero, as it were, in his relationship to God. If he dies in a fallen condition, neither Westminster theology nor Arminius grants for sure he is elected. Westminster theology theorizes that the fallen saint is never destitute of God's seed; but, like its predestinarianism as a whole, this is abstract and formal, and bears little connection to the concrete fact that the ground of assurance is godliness, and that that ground being removed removes hope.

It manifestly appears then that Westminster theology and Arminius agree that it is only the persevering believer after all who can be certainly said to be elected.

Westminster theology is thus haunted with inconsistencies. These might have been largely removed had they simply made Christ's death the ground of assurance, but positing this would have ultimately forced them to the universality of Christ's death, and Arminius had stolen that teaching from Calvinism long ago. They retained the Beza-Perkins theology with Ames' corrections. Westminster theology, then, represents a substantial departure from the thought of John Calvin. Westminster theology hardly deserves to be called Calvinistic—especially if that term is to imply the thought of Calvin himself. Perkins may not have been the first to assume that he upheld "the Calvinistic doctrine," and Warfield certainly was not the last to think that Westminster theology was Calvin's but the time is surely overdue that historical theology present a more accurate picture of what really happened between Calvin's era and that which witnessed the emergence of Westminster theology" (Kendall, pp. 211-213).

Scottish Presbyterianism

In 1982, M. Charles Bell submitted a doctoral dissertation to the University of Aberdeen, later published (1985) under the title *Calvin and Scottish Theology*. In the introduction of his book, he said, "The major thesis of this study is that whereas Calvin taught that faith is fundamentally passive in nature, is centered in the mind for understanding, is primarily to be viewed in terms of certain knowledge such that the assurance of salvation is of the essence of faith, and is grounded *extra nos*, outside ourselves and the person and work of Jesus Christ, Scottish theology, on the other hand, gradually came to teach that faith is primarily active, centered in the will or heart, and that assurance is not of the essence of faith, but is a fruit of faith, to be gathered through self examination and syllogistic deduction, thereby placing the grounds of assurance *intra nos*, within ourselves" (Bell, p. 8).

In other words, according to Bell, the same thing that happened in English Calvinism happened in Scottish Presbyterianism, the effects of which are felt until this day. As Bell points out, "It is well known, for example, that for generations many in the Scottish Highlands have refused to receive the communion elements because of the want of personal assurance of their salvation" (Bell, p. 7).

Evangelicalism

Modern evangelicalism has been extensively influenced by the Westminster Confession. Presbyterians trace their theological roots to it. The majority of Baptists trace their doctrinal position to the Second London Confession (1677), which follows the Westminster Confession almost verbatim except for statements relating to church government.

Summary: The idea that assurance is based on works and that people should examine themselves to see if the are among the elect began with Beza's teaching of limited atonement and Perkins' popularization of the use of 2 Peter 1:10.

Lordship Salvation today teaches that in order to be saved one must turn from sin and submit to the lordship of Christ. When that is done, there will be an inevitable and perceivable transformation in behavior. Assurance is based on that change. Lordship Salvationists like to claim that they are in the mainstream of historic Christianity. The truth is their position is nothing more than Puritan theology. While many within evangelicalism today have been heavily influenced by the Puritan theology and the Westminster Confession, that, by no stretch of the imagination, means that all evangelicals have or, for that matter, that the Puritan theology is Biblical. The theological heritage of Lordship Salvation in general and the view that assurance is based on sanctification in particular is not the mainstream of historic Christianity, but Puritan theology. It is rooted in hyper-Calvinism and limited atonement.

12
CONCLUSION

The current controversy concerning salvation within evangelicalism revolves around three issues: the condition (requirement) for salvation, the certainty (assurance) of salvation and the consequences (results) of salvation. All agree that salvation is by faith, but there are three different approaches to leading people to Christ and two radically different views on assurance and the results of salvation. The purpose of this "conclusion" is to succinctly summarize True Grace and Lordship Salvation, briefly answer the fundamental questions involved and address several practical cases.

True Grace

The New Testament teaches that salvation is by faith alone in Christ alone. Assurance is based on taking God at His Word; it comes with faith. When people trust Christ, they are born again; God changes them on the inside. They have spiritual life planted inside of them. Therefore, it is reasonable to expect that the inward change will manifest itself. At the same time, it is also true that for that new life to grow, it must be fed the Word of God (1 Pet. 2:1-2). Moreover, for growth to take place, believers must cooperate with the growth process (1 Pet. 2:1-2). Believers can grieve the Holy Spirit with sin (Eph. 4:30-31), hindering their growth. If believers are not fed the Word or if they do not cooperate, growth will not take place, as it should.

.

Lordship Salvation

According to Lordship Salvation advocates, God gives people faith and since God gives people faith, they will always produce perceivable, permanent fruit. Assurance is based on self-examination of one's life.

The problem with Lordship Salvation theology is that it overemphasizes God's work in believers and underemphases the believer's responsibility. To put so much emphasis on God's work without a proper focus on the human response is to miss the tenor of the New Testament. It is to fail to give a proper place to the commands of the New Testament and not take the warning of the New Testament seriously.

Actually, the Lordship Salvation interpretation of the New Testament is based on *a priori* reasoning. *A priori* (Latin: from + before) is deductive reasoning. It reasons deductively from cause to effect, from a generalization to a particular instance. According to the dictionary, it means "before examination or analysis." In other words, this approach begins with assumptions, namely that true believers always produce observable fruit and they always endure to the end.

Theology should be based on *A posteriori* reasoning. *A posteriori* (Latin: from + after) is inductive reasoning. It reasons inductively from effect to cause, from a particular instance to a generalization. According to the dictionary, it is based on observation, experience or empirical evidence. The proper method of studying the Scripture is to examine every passage in context without any preconceived ideas about what it must say.

The Specific Question

All of this raises questions such as, "Are a change in behavior, fruit and endurance automatic?" No. Granted, God works in the life of a believer, but believers are responsible to respond, including believing in Christ and obeying Him.

What is the fruit? What are works? In the New Testament, fruit is used of Christian character (Gal. 5:22-23, 2 Pet. 1:5-8), good works (Col. 1:10), converts (Rom. 1:13), praise (Heb. 13:15) and giving money (Rom. 15:28) (see Ryrie, SGS, pp. 49-50). In James 2, works include feeding the hungry and clothing the naked (Jas. 2:15-16). When self-appointed "fruit inspectors" examine the spiritual lives of others to see if the are really believers, they look for sin in someone's life. One of the major problems with that is all believers sin (Jas. 3:1, 1 Jn. 1:8, 10). These fruit inspectors usually do not look for things such as feeding the hungry and clothing the naked. In the case of James 2, the illustration of works is feeding the hungry and clothing the naked!

How much fruit is enough? In the first place, there are degrees of fruit. Jesus plainly said, "He who received seed on the good ground is he who hears the word and understands *it,* who indeed bears fruit and produces: some a hundredfold, some sixty, some thirty" (Mt. 13:23). Ryrie speaks of the evidence of fruit in the life of a believer as being "strong or weak, erratic or regular, visible or not" (Ryrie, SGS, p. 47). In his chapter on fruit, he entitles one section, "The Theory of Relativity" (Ryrie, SGS, p. 47).

The amount of fruit may be very small. MacArthur insists that all believers must bear fruit. He says, "There is no such thing as a fruitless Christian. Everyone has some fruit" (MacArthur, SWD, p, 32), but he admits, "You may have to look hard to find even a small grape, but if you look close enough, you will find something (MacArthur, SWD, p. 32). He also acknowledges, "Believers who are not fruitful go spiritually blind because their perspective is limited" (MacArthur, SWD, p, 126). Notice, he said "not fruitful!"

How far can a believer fall? In at least some ways, believers can live in such a way that their behavior is that of unsaved people (1 Cor. 3:3). Even MacArthur says that when "true Christians" fail to live a virtuous life, they are "indistinguishable from an apostate or a worldly hanger-on who leeches off the church" (MacArthur, SWD, p, 125).

Believers can fall far. They can lie, steal, commit sexual immorality (David), murder (1 Pet. 4:15), deny the Lord (Peter) and even go so far as to be a busybody (1 Pet. 4:15). No amount of sin is acceptable, but none of us have arrived (Phil. 3:12). By the way, falsely judging others is also a sin (Jas. 4:11-12).

How long can believers stay away? The answer to that, unfortunately, is the rest of their lives. They can persist in sin until the discipline of God results in their premature physical death (1 Cor. 11:30).

If a person can trust Christ, live with sin in their life and go to heaven, why live a godly life? (Before you react, remember, all believers do that to some degree. No believer is perfect, yet.) There are many answers to that question. Sin damages one's life. Living with anger destroys life, not just one's spiritual life, but the enjoyment of life period. God disciplines His children. If we judge ourselves, we avoid the judgment of God on our life (1 Cor. 11:31). God rewards those who are faithful—unto death (Rev. 2:10).

In the final analysis, some do not manifest immediate, perceivable change in behavior. There is such a thing as a secret disciple (Jn. 19:38). Some produce little, if any fruit (Jn. 15:2, 2 Pet. 1:8-9, 1 Cor. 3:11-15). Some believers are carnal (1 Cor. 3:1-3). Genuine regenerate believers can fall away (Lk. 8:13). Some do not endure, even in faith (2 Tim. 2:13). There is a sin unto death (1 Jn. 5:16, 1 Cor. 11:30, Acts 5:1-11).

Other Specific Issues

There are other verses and issues that could be addressed. Given the complexity of this subject, no one book is exhaustive. Nevertheless, one other issue that comes up, namely, church history, should at least be mentioned. Both sides want to claim support from church history (MacArthur, GAJ, pp. 221-237, FW, pp. 235-258 and Llewellen, *Bibliotheca Sacra*, Jan.-March, 1990:59).

In the first place, the issue of church history should be a non-issue. The issue is the Scripture. The purpose of this presentation is to expound the verses involved in the debate. That and only that should be the determining factor.

In the second place, the argument that the True Grace explanation is recent or that it comes from one small segment of American Christianity, even if it is true, is irrelevant. Shortly after the Protestant Reformation, that argument could have been made against the doctrine of justification by faith. It would have been irrelevant then as it is now in this controversy, because the issue is, "What does God say, not what does church history say?" MacArthur uses this argument (See MacArthur, FW, pp. 219-233) and he believes in Pretribulation rapture. The same argument he uses against True Grace is often used against Pretribulation rapture. If he wishes to suggest that True Grace be abandoned on that ground, he is forced to give up Pretribulation rapture.

Ryrie puts this issue into proper perspective when he writes, "The antiquity or recency of a teaching and the number of people who are for or against it make for interesting study, but neither factor proves or disproves the truth of that teaching. The charge of newness was leveled against the teachings of the Reformers. With characteristic straightforwardness, John Calvin responded to it this way: 'First, by calling it 'new' they do great wrong to God, whose Sacred Word does not deserve to be accused of novelty. . . . That it has lain long unknown and buried is the fault of man's impiety. Now when it is restored to us by God's goodness, its claims to antiquity ought to be admitted at least by right of recovery'" (Ryrie, SGS, p. 33).

Specific Examples

From a practical point of view, there are several possible scenarios that need to be analyzed.

First, some who make a profession of faith manifest at least some change in their life and are faithful to some degree to the end. In terms of the salvation controversy, these types of people are not an issue. Regardless of one's theological perspective, the productive professor, who has perceivable and permanent fruit, is not a problem. Such an individual does not live in gross sin, does not fall away, nor deny the faith.

A second scenario concerns those who make a profession of faith and do not show change in their life. These kinds of people are legitimate objects of concern. Only those who practice a naïve Decisionism and believe in eternal security would say categorically that such people are saved. For the Lordship Salvation advocates, this scenario is easy. Such people were never saved, because in their opinion, all believers produce immediately perceivable fruit. As has been demonstrated, the passages Lordship advocates use to support such a notion do not sustain their claim. Nevertheless, the question remains, "Do all believers produce fruit?"

Evidently, it is possible to be a believer and not produce *immediately* observable fruit. There is such a thing as a secret disciple (Jn. 19:38). Ryrie, who insists that all believers produce fruit says, "This does not mean that a certain person's fruit will necessarily be outwardly evident. Even if I know the person and have some regular contact with him, I still may not see his fruit. Indeed, I might even have legitimate grounds for wondering if he is a believer because I have not seen fruit. His fruit may be very private or erratic, but the fact that I do not see it does not mean it is not there" (Ryrie, SGS, p. 45).

Producing fruit immediately is one thing, but how about long term? There are passages that seem to suggest that it is possible for believers not to have fruit. Jesus says, "Every branch in Me that does not bear fruit He takes away" (Jn. 15:2). Jesus is speaking of saved people (cf. "in Me"), who have no fruit. Paul describes believers who have all their works burned up at the Judgment Seat of Christ (1 Cor. 3:11-15). Peter exhorts believers to add spiritual qualities to their lives (2 Pet. 1:5-7). Then, he declares, "For if these things are yours and abound, *you will be* neither barren nor unfruitful in the knowledge of our Lord Jesus Christ. For he who lacks these things is shortsighted, even to blindness, and has forgotten that he was cleansed from his old sins" (2 Pet 1:8-9; see also Titus 3:14). Notice, Peter speaks of the possibility of believers being unfruitful, that is believers lacking the fruit of the Spirit.

Each of these arguments has an answer. The point Jesus seems to be making is that when a believer does not have fruit, God the Father begins to work so that individual will produce fruit. In the context of 1 Corinthians 3, Paul is describing church leaders and their church work, but in the next chapter, he says that when the Lord returns to judge, "each one's praise will come from God" (1 Cor. 4:5), which seems to imply that every believer will be praised for something. Perhaps, it could be argued that Paul does not mean to imply that believers have no fruit whatsoever. After all, "Whom the Lord loves He chastens, and scourges every son whom He receives" (Heb. 12:6) and He does that so that "*we* may be partakers of His holiness" (Heb. 12:10).

In the final analysis, it is logical to assume that those who have been regenerated and thus have a new nature will have some fruit. Hodges writes, "Of course, there is every reason to believe that there will be good works in the life of each believer in Christ. The idea that one may believe in Him and live for years totally unaffected by the amazing miracle of regeneration, or by the instruction and/or discipline of God as heavenly Father, is a fantastic notion—even bizarre, we rejected categorically." Later in the same article he says, "We said earlier that we believe that all born-again Christians will do good works. We believe, however, because it appears to be the only rational inference from the scriptural data. But, let it be said clearly, it is an inference. No text of Scripture (certainly not Jas 2:14-26!) declares that all believers will perform good works, much less that they cannot be sure of heaven unless they do. No text says that!" (Hodges, *Journal of the Grace Evangelical Society*, vol. 3, Num.

2, pp. 3-17; see pp. 7-9). In his book, *Absolutely Free*, Hodge writes, "It is wrong to claim that a life of dedicated obedience is guaranteed by regeneration, or even that such works as there are must be visible to a human observer. God alone may be able to detect the fruit of regeneration in some of His children" (Hodges, AF, p. 215).

Ryrie insists, "Every Christian will bear spiritual fruit. Somewhere, sometime, somehow" (Ryrie, SGS, p. 45. Also "Good works always accompany salvation," in a note on Eph. 2:8 in the *Ryrie Study Bible*), but he warns, "My understanding of what is fruit is and therefore what I expect others to bear may be faulty and/or incomplete. It is too easy to have a mental list of spiritual fruit and to conclude someone does not produce what is on my list that he or she is not a believer. But the reality is that most lists that we humans devise are too short, too selective, too prejudiced and often extrabiblical" (Ryrie, SGS, pp. 45-46). Ryrie goes on to argue that even a person who dies immediately after receiving Christ produces fruit. He points out that when anyone is converted, he experience peace with God (peace is a fruit of the Spirit) and there is joy in heaven (joy is a fruit of the Spirit) (Ryrie, SGS, p. 46). He concludes, "So likely it can truly be said that every believer will bear fruit somewhere (in earth and/or heaven), sometime (regularly and/or irregularly during life), somehow (publicly and/or privately)" (Ryrie, SGS, p. 46).

The real dispute is over a third scenario. What about those make a profession of faith, manifest some change in their life and fall into sin or fall away from the faith? This scenario consists of several subgroups.

1.   Some profess faith in Christ, produce some fruit, but practice sin. Is it possible for a genuine Christian to live like that? What should be our attitude and approach to such individuals?

The simple reality is the New Testament recognizes that believers can be carnal. Paul told the Corinthians they were carnal, that is, "babes in Christ" (1 Cor. 3:1). He goes on to charge them with "behaving like *mere* men?" (1 Cor. 3:3), meaning unsaved men! In comment on this passage, Ryrie says, "To be sure, Christians are not supposed to live like unsaved people, but the reality is that some do. For how long? More than a moment or a day or a month or a year? When Paul wrote 1 Corinthians, those believers were four or five years old in the faith, and obviously some of them were still carnal or fleshly" (Ryrie, SGS, p. 31).

In the case of 1 Corinthians 3, the sins mentioned are envy, strife, and divisions (1 Cor. 3:3). It can get worse. In 1 Corinthians 5, Paul says, "It is actually reported *that there is* sexual immorality among you, and such sexual immorality as is not even named among the Gentiles; that a man has his father's wife!" (1 Cor 5:1). This believer (1 Cor. 5:5) was living in immorality with his stepmother! In 1 Timothy 5, Paul suggests that it is possible for a believer to do something worse that an unbeliever. He says, "But if anyone does not provide for his own, and especially for those of his household, he has denied the faith and is worse than an unbeliever" (1 Tim. 5:8).

Peter contemplates the possibility of a believer being guilty of murder. In fact, he says, "But let none of you suffer as a murderer, a thief, an evildoer, or as a busybody in other people's matters" (1 Pet. 4:15). Ryrie says, "Does he mean that a believer could be a troublesome meddler? To answer yes seems not too difficult. Does he mean a believer could be an evildoer? Again we can be comfortable with a yes answer. Does he mean a believer could be a thief? Perhaps it becomes a little more difficult to say yes, except we remember that Paul also said believers steal (Ephesians 4:28). But does Peter mean a believer could commit murder? If so, this surely seems to be the depths of carnality." He adds, "Commentators do not hesitate to acknowledge that believers can be guilty of any of these crimes listed in verse 15" (Ryrie, SGS, pp. 64-65).

2.   Some profess faith in Christ, manifest some fruit and later fall away. In these cases, they cease gathering with the assembly of believers. It is not that they live an overtly sinful lifestyle; they may live a relatively moral life apart from attending church services. Is it possible for genuine believers to do that? What should our attitude and approach be toward them?

As we have seen, Jesus speaks of people "who believe for a while and in time of temptation fall away" (Lk. 8:13). The Greek word translated "temptation" means, "trial, temptation." In Luke 8, it is a reference to a trial, not a temptation. Matthew's account says, "tribulation or persecution arises because of the word" (Mt. 13:21). Mark's account says, "tribulation or persecution arises for the word's sake" (Mk. 4:17). The trial is persecution because of the Word. Because of persecution, some fall away. That does not means they live in gross sin.

The Greek word translated "fall away" in Luke 8:13 is also used in Hebrews 8:12, which says, "Beware, brethren, lest there be in any of you an evil heart of unbelief in departing from the living God" (Heb. 3:12). In the case of the book of Hebrews, Jewish believers were contemplating returning to Judaism. Falling away was not falling into what we think of as a sinful lifestyle; it was living a moral, religious lifestyle, apart from Christianity.

3. Some profess faith in Christ, manifest some fruit, and later deny the faith. They ceased to believe the basic facts of the Christian faith. As has been pointed out, it is possible for Christians to deny the faith (2 Tim. 2:13).

The New Testament seems to indicate that some believers do not begin well, some live carnal lives all their life and some don't end up too well. That's tragic, but true. When it happens we should be grieved and do everything we can to help those believers grow. I would personally begin by going over the truths of the gospel to make sure the individual is saved. Once I was satisfied he or she understood the gospel and gave a clear testimony of having trusted Christ, I would urge that individual by the mercies of God to grow in the grace and knowledge of Jesus Christ.

Summary: Lordship Salvation is not Biblical and creates a number of practical problems.

Lordship Salvation causes confusion concerning the requirement for eternal life. It produces unnecessary doubts in the minds of believers about the assurance of eternal life. It result is a judgmental attitude among many of those who adopt it.

We need to proclaim the free grace of God. Sinners are saved by God's grace. Ryrie is right when he says. "The Gospel is the good news of the grace of God to give forgiveness and eternal life. Let's keep the gospel so full of grace that there is no room for anything else to dilute or pollute the true grace of God" (Ryrie, SGS, p. 18).

Saints are sanctified by the grace of God. They need to be taught to not fall short of the grace of God (Heb. 12:15), to go to the throne of grace for grace to help in the time of need (Heb. 4:16) and grow in the grace and knowledge of Jesus Christ (2 Pet. 3:18). That is the true grace of God.

BIBLIOGRAPHY

Abbott-Smith, G., *A Manual Greek Lexicon of the New Testament*. Edinburgh: T & T. Clark, 1960.

Alexander, Joseph Addison, *Commentary on the Acts of the Apostles*, 2 vols. Grand Rapids: Zondervan Publishing House, 1956.

Alexander, Joseph Addison, *The Gospel According to Matthew*. Minneapolis: James Family Christian Publishers, 1861.

Alford, Henry, *The Greek Testament*. Chicago: Moody Press, 1968.

Bietenhard, Hans, "Lord," *Theological Dictionary of the New Testament*, eds., Kittel, G. and Bromiley G. W., Grand Rapids: Wm. B. Eerdmans, 1967.

Bell, M. Charles, *Calvin and Scottish Theology*. Edinburgh: The Handsel Press, 1985.

Berkhof, L., *Systematic Theology*. Grand Rapids: Wm. B. Eerdmans Publishing, 1961.

Brooke, A. E., *A Critical and Exegetical Commentary of the Johannine Epistles*. New York: Charles Scribner's Sons: 1928.

Bromiley, Geoffery W., "Faith," *International Standard Bible Encyclopedia*, Rev. Ed. 4 vols. Grand Rapids: Wm. B. Eerdmans Publishing, 1980-1988.

Brown, Colin, ed. *The New International Dictionary of New Testament Theology*, 2 vols. Grand Rapids: Zondervan Publishing House, 1976.

Bruce, F. F., *The Book of Acts*. Grand Rapids: William B. Eerdmans, 1989.

Bruce, F. F., *The Gospel of John*. Grand Rapids: Wm. B. Eerdmans Publishing, 1983.

Calvin, John, *The Institutes of the Christian Religion*. Grand Rapids: Associated Publishers and Authors, n. d.

Calvin, John, Calvin's Bible *Commentaries*. Ages Software. www.ageslibrary.com

Cairns, Earle E., *Christianity Through the Centuries*. Zondervan Publishing House, 1981.

Chafer, Lewis Sperry, *Systematic Theology*. Dallas: Dallas Theological Seminary, 1948.

Chafer, Lewis Sperry, *The Ephesian Letter*. Findlay, Ohio: Dunham Publishing Co., 1935.

Cocoris, G. Michael, *Evangelism: A Biblical Approach*. Chicago: Moody Press, 1984.

Cocoris, G. Michael, "John MacArthur, Jr.'s System of Salvation" (1989). Available under Topical studies at insightsfromtheword.com.

Cocoris, G. Michael, *Lordship Salvation: Is it Biblical?* Dallas: Redencion Viva, 1983.

Cocoris, G. Michael, *Repentance: the Most Misunderstood Word in the Bible* (2003). Available under Topical Studies at insightsfromtheword.com.

Creed, John Martin, *The Gospel According to St. Luke*. London: Macmillan & Co. Ltd, 1965.

Dibelius, Martin, *James*, Philadelphia: Fortress Press, 1976.

Dillow, Joseph C., *The Reign of the Servant Kings*. Miami Springs: Schoettle Publishing Co. 1992.

Eadie, John, *Commentary on the Epistle to the Ephesians*. Grand Rapids: Zondervan Publishing House, 1883.

Eadie, John, *Commentary on the Greek Text of the Epistle of Paul to the Philippians*. Edinburgh: T. & T. Clark, 1884.

Enlow, Elmer R., "Eternal Life: On What Conditions?" *Alliance Witness*, January 19, 1972.

Erickson, Millard J., *Christian Theology*. Grand Rapids: Baker Book House, 1990.

France, R. T., *Matthew, The Tyndale Bible Commentaries*. Grand Rapids: William B. Eerdmans, 1983

Fromer, Paul, "The Real Issue in Salvation." *His,* June, 1958.

Geldenhuys, Norval, *Commentary on Luke*, The New International Commentary Series. Grand Rapids: Eerdmans, 1983.

Gingrich, F. Wilbur and Frederick W. Danker, eds., *A Greek-English Lexicon of the New Testament and Other Early Christian Literature*, 2nd ed. Chicago: The University of Chicago Press, 1979.

Gloag, Paton J., *A Critical and Exegetical Commentary on the Acts of the Apostles*. Minnesota: Klock & Klock Christian Publishers, 1979.

Godet, F. L., *Commentary on the Epistles to the Romans.* Grand Rapids: Zondervan Publishing House, 1956.

Godet, F. L., *Commentary on the Gospel of John.* 2 vols. Grand Rapids: Zondervan Publishing House, 1883.

Godet, F. L., *Commentary on the Gospel of St. Luke.* 2 vols. Grand Rapids: Zondervan Publishing House, 1887.

Govett, Robert, *Govett on John.* Miami Springs, Florida: Conley & Schoettle Publishing Co., Inc., 1984.

Guthrie, Donald, *Hebrews*, The Tyndale Bible Commentaries. Grand Rapids: William B. Eerdmans, 1986.

Hodge, Charles, *A Commentary on the Epistle to the Ephesians*. London: The Banner of Truth Trust, 1964.

Hodge, Charles, *A Commentary on the Epistle to the Romans*. Grand Rapids: Wm. B. Eerdmans Publishing, 1976.

Hodges, Zane, C., "1 John," *The Bible Knowledge Commentary*, ed. John F. Walvoord, Roy B. Zuck. Wheaton: Victor Books, 1983.

Hodges, Zane C., *Absolutely Free*. Grand Rapids: Zondervan Publishing House, 1989.

Hodges, Zane C., *The Epistles of John*. Irving, Texas: Grace Evangelical Society, 1999.

Hodges, Zane, C., *The Gospel Under Siege*. Dallas: Redencion Viva, 1981.

Hodges, Zane, C., "Hebrews," *The Bible Knowledge Commentary*, ed. John F. Walvoord, Roy B. Zuck. Wheaton: Victor Books, 1983.

Hodges, Zane C., "Problem Passages in the Gospel of John Part II, Untrustworthy Believers—John 2:23-25." *Bibliotheca Sacra*, April, 1978, vol. 135, pp. 140-153.

Hodges, Zane C., "We Believe In: Assurance of Salvation," *Journal of the Grace Evangelical Society*, vol. 3, num. 2.

Hogan, William, "The Relationship of the Lordship of Christ to Salvation" (Ph.D. dissertation. Wheaton College, Wheaton, Ill., 1958.

Inglis, James, "Simon Magus." *Journal of the Grace Evangelical Society*, Spring 1989, vol. 2:1.

Ironside, H. I., *Full Assurance*. Chicago: Moody Press, 1968.

Jamieson, Robert, A. R. Fausset, and David Brown, *A Commentary, Critical Experimental and Practical on the Old and New Testaments*. Grand Rapids: William B. Eerdmans Publishing Co., 1961.

Kendall, R. T., *Calvin and English Calvinism to 1649*. Oxford: Oxford University Press, 1979.

Kendall, R. T., *Once Saved, Always Saved*. Chicago: Moody Press, 1985.

Kent, Jr., Homer A., *The Pastoral Epistles*. Chicago: Moody Press, 1958.

Kent, Jr., Homer A., *The Epistle to the Hebrews*. Grand Rapids: Baker Book House, 1974.

Liddell, H. G. and Scott R., *An Intermediate Greek-English Lexicon*. New York: Harper & Brothers Publishers, 1894.

Lightfoot, J. B., *Notes on the Epistles of St. Paul*. London: MacMillan, 1895.

Litfin, A. Duane, "2 Timothy," *The Bible Knowledge Commentary*, ed. John F. Walvoord, Roy B. Zuck. Wheaton: Victor Books, 1983.

Llewellen, Thomas G., "Has Lordship Salvation Been Taught throughout Church History?" *Bibliotheca Sacra*, Jan.-March, 1990:59.

MacArthur, Jr., John F., *The Gospel According to Jesus.* Grand Rapids: Zondervan Publishing House, 1988.

MacArthur, Jr., John F., *Faith Works.* Dallas: Word Publishing, 1993.

MacArthur, Jr., John F., *Saved Without a Doubt.* Colorado Springs: Chariot Victor Publishing, 1992.

McDonald, William, Believer's *Bible Commentary.* Nashville: Thomas Nelson Publishers, 1990.

Machen, J. Gresham, *The Origin of Paul's Religion.* New York: The MacMillan Co., 1921.

Machen, J. Gresham, *What is Faith?* Grand Rapids: William B. Eerdmans Publishing Company, 1925.

Mantey, Julius R. "Repentance and Conversion" in *Basic Christian Doctrine*, edited by Carl F. H. Henry. New York: Holt Rinehart and Winston, 1962.

Marshall, I. Howard, *Acts*, Tyndale New Testament Commentaries. Grand Rapids: William B. Eerdmans, 1986.

Marshall, I. Howard, *The Epistles of John*, The New International Commentary on the New Testament. Grand Rapids: William B. Eerdmans, 1984.

Martin, Ralph P., *The Epistle of Paul to the Philippians.* Tyndale New Testament Commentaries. Grand Rapids: William B. Eerdmans, 1983.

Mitchell, G. John, *An Everlasting Love: A Devotional Study of the Gospel of John.* Portland: Multnomah Press, 1982.

Morris, Leon, *The Gospel According to John.* Grand Rapids: William B. Eerdmans, 1984.

Muller, Jac. J., *The Epistle of Paul to the Philippians.* Grand Rapids: William B. Eerdmans, 1984.

Moulton, James Hope and Milligan, George, *The Vocabulary of the Greek Testament.* Grand Rapids: Wm. B. Eerdmans Publishing Company, 1972.

Murray, John, *The Epistle to the Romans*, The New International Commentary on the New Testament. Grand Rapids: William B. Eerdmans, 1968.

Packer, J. I., *Evangelism and the Sovereignty of God*. Chicago: Inter-Varsity Press, 1961.

Plummer, Alfred, *A Critical and Exegetical Commentary on the First Epistle of St Paul to the Corinthians*. New York: Charles Scribner's Sons, 1920.

Plummer, Alfred, *A Critical and Exegetical Commentary on the Second Epistle of the St Paul to the Corinthians*. New York: Charles Scribner's Sons, 1915.

Plummer, Alfred, *The Epistles of St. John*, The Cambridge Bible for School and Colleges. Cambridge: The University Press, 1892.

Plummer, Alfred, *An Exegetical Commentary on the Gospel According to St. Matthew*. Minneapolis: James Family Christian Publishers, n. d.

Plummer, Alfred, *The General Epistles of St. James and St. Jude*. New York: A. C. Armstrong and Son, 1905.

Plummer, Alfred, *The Gospel According to St. John*, The Cambridge Bible for School and Colleges. Cambridge: The University Press, 1902.

Plummer, Alfred, *The Gospel According to St. Luke*, International Critical Commentary Series. New York: Charles Scribner's Sons, 1903.

Rackham, Richard Belward, *The Acts of the Apostles*. London: Metuen & Co LTD, 1957.

Robertson, A. T., *Word Pictures in the Greek New Testament*. 6 vols. Nashville: Boardman, 1933.

Robinson, Haddon W. *The Solid Rock Construction Company*. Grand Rapids: Discovery House Publishers, 1989.

Robinson, J. Armitage, *St. Paul's Epistle to the Ephesians*. London: James Clarke & Co. LTD, n. d.

Ryrie, Charles C., *Basic Theology*. Wheaton, Illinois: Victor Books, 1986.

Ryrie, Charles C., *So Great Salvation*. Wheaton, Illinois: Victor Books, 1989.

Ryrie, Charles C., *A Bible Doctrine*. Chicago: Moody Press, 1972.

Sandy, W. and Headlam, A. C., *The Epistles to the Romans*. New York: Charles Scribner's Sons, 1923.

Saucy, Robert L., "The Presence of the Kingdom and the Life of the Church," *Bibliotheca Sacra*, January, 1988: 124.

Smalley, S. Stephen, *Word Biblical Commentary, 1, 2, 3, John*. Waco, Texas: Word Books Publisher, 1984.

Stott, John R., "Must Christ be Lord to be Savior?-Yes," *Eternity*, September, 1959.

Stott, John R., *The Epistles of John*, The Tyndale Bible Commentaries. Grand Rapids: William B. Eerdmans, 1964.

Swete, Henry Barclay, *The Gospel According to St. Mark*. Grand Rapids: Wm. B. Eerdmans Publishing, 1956.

Tasker, R. V. G., *Matthew*, The Tyndale Bible Commentaries. Grand Rapids: William B. Eerdmans, 1983.

Torrey, R. A., *What the Bible Teaches*. New York: Revell, 1898.

Trench, Richard Chenevix, *Synonyms of the New Testament*. Grand Rapids: Eerdmans, 1963.

Westcott, B. F., *The Epistles of St. John*, Grand Rapids: William B. Eerdmans, 1966.

Westcott, B. F., *The Epistle to the Hebrews*. Grand Rapids: William B. Eerdmans, 1965.

Warfield, Benjamin B., *The Lord of Glory*. New York: American Tract Society, 1927.

Wiersbe, Warren W., *Be Loyal*. Wheaton: Victor Books, 1980.